The Vanished World of Robert Youngson

The Vanished World of Robert Youngson

by Jim Manago

BearManor Media
2018

The Vanished World of Robert Youngson

© 2018 Jim Manago

All rights reserved.

For information, address:

BearManor Media
P. O. Box 71426
Albany, GA 31708

bearmanormedia.com

Typesetting and layout by John Teehan

Published in the USA by BearManor Media

ISBN—978-1-62933-380-9

In memory of my friend Joe Franklin.

Table of Contents

Acknowledgements ix

Introduction 1

Part One: Robert Youngson's Life

1 The Curtain Rises on the Star 7
2 Bob on the Shorts 11
3 Enter Jeanne and Al 17
4 Film, Food and Friends 25
5 Bob on the Features 39
6 The Curtain Lowers, Hail and Farewell 43

Part Two: Robert Youngson's Films

7 Before His Independence 51
8 The Comedy Compilations 57
9 The Breakthrough 63
10 Bob Called It His Best 81
11 With Added Thrills 91

12	The Fun Continues 99
13	The Sound Disappointment 103
14	The Fiddle and the Bow 107
15	The Return of the Fiddle and the Bow 111
16	The End of the Rope 117
17	Afterword 121

Appendix:

Bibliography 125
Cameo and Puzzums 127
Awards 131
Credits 133

Acknowledgements

TRULY THE ONE PERSON that made this book a reality is Robert Youngson's wife, Jeanne Keyes Youngson. Without her assistance and openness about Bob, this book would have remained an unfulfilled dream for me.

I am indebted to Leonard Maltin for offering his priceless 1971 interview with Youngson. In addition, I must thank Brent Walker for his excellent scholarly published study, which tracked down titles to the clips used by Youngson. In addition, I am indebted to a dedicated assistant Randy Bonneville for compiling the credits. Thanks to Stephen Cox for all images, except where indicated otherwise. Special thanks must also go to Scott MacGillivray for allowing me to quote generously from his fine revised study *Laurel & Hardy: From the Forties Forward*, and (along with John McElwee) for supplying the ad mats.

From Jeanne I learned that Kent State University had received Bob's personal collection of 1,113 Pathé newsreel films on 16mm from his wife over twenty years ago (a veritable goldmine). My contact with them facilitated the correct listing on their website. Unfortunately, for some reason they neglected to make the films available to researchers. Sad to say, these films may very well be on the verge of disintegration. Perhaps, this study will encourage them to take immediate and appropriate action to make that generous donation available in the near future to researchers and visitors.

My personal assistant in all these endeavors throughout the years has been Donna Manago. Her help has been particularly important to me, and I am most thankful for her research and support.

Introduction

MY LOVE OF SILENT MOVIES started back when I became aware of them in the late 1960s and 1970s with the viewing of several of producer Robert Youngson's superb compilations on local New York television. I particularly remember seeing the first three of them a number of times; that is, *The Golden Age of Comedy*, *When Comedy Was King*, and *Days of Thrills and Laughter*. Although I spent endless hours discovering the vast world of movies on television, Youngson's motion pictures stood out so much that they enthralled me. I became awestruck and appreciative of the sheer variety of superb comedy players that were around so long before I was born. I learned that his films revived interest in the silent film comedies.

Fast forward forty years plus, and I am immersed in the world of researching and writing biographies of actors and actresses; including Shirley Booth, Huntz Hall, Kay Aldridge, Gale Gordon, and Leo Gorcey. As I sought a subject for my next biographical work. I wanted it to be about the one person that I really knew so little about but always wanted to know more about.

So much has been, and continues to be, written about actors, actresses, and (thanks to the influence of the auteur theory) directors. As you know, if any particular persons seem totally forgotten, it has been the writers and producers. I knew once I started on my authorship of books that someday I wanted to tackle this project regardless of whether anyone else saw it as worthwhile. I also knew that my interest in and respect for Youngson never waned over the years, and I personally wanted to know what made him want to make his truly haunting compilations of bygone silent comedies.

It seemed to be just a dream that might have been a possible project that someone would undertake. One day in 2015, something possessed me to look into the fantastic possibility of doing this study now so many years later. Happily, I discovered that Youngson's widow Jeanne was alive and more than willing to help me.

To my surprise, the opportunity to contact her appeared out of nowhere, with the help of Jean Shepherd's biographer, Eugene Bergmann. To my delight, Youngson's wife first replied to my query, saying, "This could be fun." In short, Jeanne immediately answered my many questions and offered stories and facts about her nearly fifteen years of married life with Youngson. In no time my book was well off and running.

I knew of film scholar William K. Everson's tribute to Youngson, in which he best described him when he said, "Robert G. Youngson, who died in April of 1974 in his early fifties, was hardly a documentarian in the strictest sense of the word. While he did occasionally shoot new material, he worked mainly from existing material, and in exhuming the past, he preserved and recorded it with affection, accuracy and humor. He had a tremendous respect for the past – a respect tinged with but not dominated by nostalgia for it – and he hated with a vengeance those films that kidded and ridiculed the past for easy quick laughs."

The world that producer/writer Youngson sought to celebrate in seven of the eight compilations all share one thing, and that is, their insistent celebration of the silent film comedies and the comedians of 1920s. Most importantly, and often misunderstood, is his intelligent and humorous comments spoken over the film excerpts. This need for narration came from Youngson's experience as a writer and producer of newsreel shorts in the 1940s and 1950s. Simply put, the narrations in his compilations gave him a chance to express his deep appreciation and familiarity of the era to the viewers.

I had heard over the years, perhaps from diehard silent film purists that Youngson ruined the original films by cutting and splicing them for his compilations. However, that is nonsensical for if it was not for his compilations (especially the first few), viewers would not have come to discover and long for these forgotten comedies. That alone would rescue these talented comics/performers from obscurity. Youngson's films reintroduced the public back in the late 1950s and 1960s to the silent comedies; these comics have had a new life. The result is that many other individuals have come to love them so much.

Youngson's compilations have been particularly instrumental in reviving interest in Laurel and Hardy; especially as far as making the world aware of their silent productions. So many people then first became aware of the team's hidden comedy treasures.

Everson: "Bob was undoubtedly responsible for the tremendous (and well-deserved) resurgence of interest in Laurel and Hardy in the 1950s; more importantly, his use of so much material, from original negatives then on the verge of decomposition, undoubtedly saved it.

"The same can be said for so much of the great newsreel footage that he unearthed, much of which is amazing for its pictorial style and beauty as much as for its content. Once unearthed by Bob, it soon became absorbed into many standard libraries, anthologies, and TV documentaries. Even if his own use of it had been less than expert than it was, his salvaging of it would have been a major contribution."

Although none of Youngson's compilations received awards, he did deserve recognition for at least one of his first three compilations. Earlier, two of his many short subjects garnered Academy Awards, as well as being nominated for three others. His skill developed with his work as a newsreel writer; the latter job acting as his training ground. Here I have steered clear of discussing this part of Youngson's career in detail because it is esoteric, as well as the fact that those productions are not accessible to all but the film scholar seeing them at an archival center.

I am grateful to Youngson for finding and bringing to his compilations so many memorable scenes; just a brief sampling of a few of my favorite selections from the first three films reveal his fine ability at sifting through literally thousands of films from that period to find some of the best silent comedy scenes ever made.

For starters, in Youngson's first compilation, *The Golden Age of Comedy*, there is excerpted the oyster stew gag (*Wandering Willies*) with the now-forgotten comedy great Billy Bevan that inspired sound comedians later, such as Lou Costello, to play the same gag. In fact, the often-overlooked Bevan receives attention in all of the first four compilations. Also, we meet the truly unforgettable Puzzums the Cat winning a game of checkers against Andy Clyde (*His Unlucky Night*), as well as the Cameo the Wonder Dog helping Bevan in a poker game and for contacting the police (*Nip and Tuck*).

In Youngson's second compilation, *When Comedy Was King*, there is some fine moments of survival for the lovers Fatty Arbuckle and Mabel Normand (*Fatty and Mabel Adrift*); and, of course, the famous "Phantom Kiss." Here Arbuckle tenderly offered what we see as a silhouetted kiss to the sleeping Normand. In addition, there is Harry Langdon acting terrified in a supposed haunted house (*His First 100 Years*), and Snub Pollard's unusual inventions to make his life easy (*It's A Gift*).

In his third compilation, *Days of Thrills and Laughter*, again we see the cute and funny Cameo the Wonder Dog. He drinks hard cider and smokes. Besides, this time he beats Ben Turpin playing a game of checkers (*Asleep at the Switch*), as well as such amazing fast-paced footage of comedian Monte Banks on a moving train (*Play Safe*).

In short, Youngson's passionate love of the silent comedies led to his making of films that made audiences aware of the existence of these forgotten shorts. Youngson's compilations opened a completely new world for them. Whether he did it for a love that he himself had of that era, and/or a belief that audiences would enjoy them, it did not matter. He managed to make it possible for millions to see these gems.

I am truly appreciative of the fact that he took the chance and went forward with his dream, even when big studios expressed disinterest, for it meant that we now have forever a group of films that unforgettably capture a world that is no longer imaginable. When I told Jeanne of the proposed title to this book, she acknowledged that it truly is a vanished world.

Part One

Robert Youngson's Life

1

The Curtain Rises on the Star

"There was a time when you could stand outside any movie theater in the land and hear peals of laughter coming through the doors. It was the day of visual comedy, now a forgotten art. Along the way we've lost laughter and something is lacking in our lives."

– Robert Youngson quoted by
Hedda Hopper, May 24, 1960

THE FAMILY TREE of Robert George Youngson (hereinafter referred to as Youngson or as Bob) can be easily traced back to his grandfather George Neils Youngson (1864 – 1930) married to Cora Belle Hill (1870 – 1952). The couple gave birth to five children; Isaac Hill Youngson (February 21, 1891- January 8, 1967), George N. Youngson, Jr. (1894 – 1985), Helen Marie Youngson (1896 – 1976), Harriet Ruth Youngson (1896 – 1957?), and Jane Alice Youngson (1911 –1995).

Youngson's father Isaac was the oldest child of his parents George and Cora. At 24 years-old, Isaac Hill Youngson, known first by the nickname of "Ike" and later as "Jack," was born in Nebraska in the town of Minden in Kearney County. Later, he would see his name credited in his son's films as "I. Hill Youngson." Jack would marry the 22-year old Caroline Deringer (1893-1961), referred to simply as "Carrie," on March 25, 1915. The couple moved shortly thereafter to Sussex, New Jersey, where they gave birth to Robert George Youngson on November 27, 1917.

His closest and dearest survivor, his wife Jeanne Keyes forty years after his untimely passing, best tells the story of Youngson. Unless otherwise noted, the following is the story from her memories of Bob using her own words.

For starters, Jeanne reminded me, "My mom's name is Margaret, which is my first name, but I've always been called Jeanne."

Youngson's parents were born and raised in a small city in Nebraska. Jeanne: "Minden, maybe. His mother came from a well-to-do family and they went to Europe when she was young. His father was Ike Youngson and when Carrie started going with him, did not like the name "Ike" – and renamed him Jack. How or why they came to Brooklyn – who knows? Maybe they just wanted to get outta Nebraska. They were Protestants but I never knew them to go to church.

"I believe his family had been in Nebraska forever. No English background at all.

Youngson – the name is Danish which means that Ike or Jack's family had probably came from there.

First off, "Everyone called him Bob," noted Jeanne. "Bob was the apple of his parents' eyes from birth. [His sister] Daris (Tonini) told me the reason she married young was to get out of the house since Bob was 'The Star.'

Jeanne explained: "The fact is that He must have had a wonderful childhood. Even at his father's funeral Bob's sister Daris came from California, and at the funeral also told my sister the reason she married at 18 was to get out of the house as she was a third class citizen and Bob was a god. As far as Bob's sister, Jeanne acknowledged there was "a couple of year's difference, I'd guess. She ran hot and cold.

"His dad Jack wore Bob's new shoes to break them in so they wouldn't hurt his feet. And one of his dad's favorite stories was how, when Bob was at Harvard, he got other guys to wait on him; [he was] a real Tom Sawyer figure. I gathered that he went to school to please his folks, but his heart was always in movies."

What is obvious then is the likely answer to the question of why Youngson made films compiling comedy footage from 1920s films. As Youngson reached the age of thirteen by 1930, his pre-adolescent years were lived in the 1920's. Since he had a very pleasant childhood, he obviously wanted to revisit it somehow.

Jeanne knew that Bob's parents (Jack and Carrie) had treated him quite well as a child. Jeanne: "I guess we'd all be nostalgic for our childhood eras if we were treated royally, especially to the exclusion of a sibling."

Interestingly Youngson was born on November 27, 1917, and he shares the same day of birth as film critic, novelist, film scriptwriter, and poet James Agee (1909). Another connection between the two men is that Agee most importantly revived the public's nostalgic interest and discussion of silent film comedy with his famous 1949 *Life* essay, "Comedy's Greatest Era." Eight years later, Youngson's film, *The Golden Age of Comedy*, would likewise cause an unparalleled interest in silent film comedy entailing six more feature-length compilations focused on showing the actual clips from the silent films.

In addition, Agee's influence on Youngson is clearly evident when Youngson's narration in several of the compilations uses lines from Agee's famous essay, at least once crediting him directly, but at other times merely appropriating Agee's actual words.

Though there are many differences between the two men, some additional similarities seem startling. Although Youngson did not have Agee's struggles with alcohol and tobacco, Youngson did have another struggle just as serious and dangerous. That is, he struggled with an obesity problem most of his adult life, which he truly seemed to ignore in one way or another.

An essay on Agee by critic Erling Larsen offers a simple description of Agee's attitude towards himself that clearly applies to Youngson as well. Larsen: "...he abused his body rather than took care of it."

Also true is that both Agee and Youngson died prematurely and, in a way, tragically due to ongoing health problems. Neither reached normal old age or even came close to retirement age. Agee had suffered heart attacks several times, and he died in a taxicab of a heart attack while heading to his doctor on May 16, 1955. Agee was six months short of his 46th birthday.

Youngson died comatose in the hospital after enduring some serious complications due to his obesity and advanced diabetes. He was seven months shy of his 57th birthday when he departed on April 15, 1974.

What is more important than the fact that they both shared short lives is that Larsen's conclusion about Agee strikingly applies to Youngson. Larsen: "...it seems clear that Agee did during his life what he wanted to.... And the work produced during this life proves that he must have achieved some 'genuine happiness.'" Indeed Youngson loved nothing more than watching and making movies and the fact that he indulged so much in overeating as if it did not truly matter indicates he did so because he lived and thrived in a perpetual state of "genuine happiness."

He was doing what he always wanted to do – watch and make films. His seeming neglect of his own mortality and his insistently fearless pursuit of living his life to the fullest and satisfying his enormous appetite left him in a terrible vulnerability to an irreversible fact. It serves as a lesson for all of us. Inevitably, it is certain fact that unresolved obesity will shorten one's lifespan regardless of how good you are or how wonderful your contribution to humanity is.

2

Bob on the Shorts

"There was a period of time in which there was a feeling that silent films had no commercial value whatsoever. If I may be immodest, I think I had more to do with disproving that than anyone else. It was heartbreaking, there were so many films I wanted to get from the Warner library which had completely been destroyed."

– Robert Youngson, 1971 Interview,
Film Fan Monthly

IN A RARE 1971 INTERVIEW with a fanzine called *Film Fan Monthly* (*FFM*), edited by Leonard Maltin, Youngson answered questions in his New York apartment, surrounded by movie items, including his two Academy Awards. What we are fortunate to have is Youngson's own words preserved which best tell of how he came to be the producer and writer of newsreel and movie shorts for Warner-Pathé.

Maltin recalled, "I didn't know Bob well... I believe I met him through our mutual friend, the film historian and teacher William K. Everson. When I approached him about conducting an interview, he couldn't have been more gracious or welcoming. He lived in an enormous apartment at – I think – #1 Fifth Avenue near Washington Square, if my memory isn't failing me completely. Whenever I visited there was a fellow there helping him out named Al, who turned out to be Alfred Dahlem. He's credited on most of the features, but I never really knew if he was Bob's helper, housekeeper, or jack of all trades."

The *FFM* interview began by asking Youngson to pinpoint his initial interest in movies. Youngson responded: "Oh, it began when I was a child. I always had a tremendous interest in motion picture history, and the motion picture past. Back when I was a kid, we didn't have the Museum of Modern Art, and we didn't have any place to see old films, really. I used to rent films from Willoughby's, which had a film rental library. They had a lot of good things. Very good old silent comedies and beautiful prints. That's where I got to see my first old films. Unfortunately, none of my friends had the slightest interest in old silent movies. So I would have to figure out all ways of enticing them over to my place to see these old movies. It was sort of a lonely hobby.

"How it ever started I don't know, except that the interest was there from the very beginning, sort of inborn. It wasn't fanned by anybody because there was no one to fan it at that time. Then shortly thereafter the Museum of Modern Art began operation, and it was just wonderful; they had all original prints – Griffith had donated all his original prints and Fairbanks. Most of those old original prints, I believe, are now all hypoed and gone, and they show reproductions, which are not the same because you don't have your tints and your tones. These being prints owned by the people who made the films, they were perfect."

When asked how his interest in films turned into a career, Youngson explained: "How it all began was in high school; I made a bunch of amateur motion pictures. I went to Harvard Business School and the Harvard Film Society had a contest; I entered a film that I had made in high school. It won first prize, so I sat down and wrote all the motion picture companies, hoping I might get a nibble somewhere along the line.

"A man named Fred Ullman, who was the head of what was then RKO, had me in for an interview, and gave me a job; so I went right from Harvard Business School [he graduated in 1941] into RKO-Pathé working as a newsreel contact man, which meant I had to go out with newsreel crews, arrange stories; then later on I became a script writer for the Pathé newsreel.

"Well, this all began in 1941, so I became scriptwriter for Pathé News about 1942. During the War, I was sent down to a Naval Air Station in Jacksonville, Florida to write naval training films, as a Pathé employee. Then I came back and continued to write newsreels, and did freelance writing on the outside. Then, under most fortunate circumstances, RKO-Pathé was purchased by Warner Brothers, and it became Warner-Pathé.

"There was a very great and perceptive man named Norman Moray, who was made the head of Warner-Pathé. He was also the sales manager of all the Warners Brothers Shorts. He was a very friendly man, and one day, I was walking down the hall and this brisk, friendly, gray-haired man stopped me and introduced himself. I told him who I was, and what I did, and he invited me to lunch.

"At lunch I told him an idea that I had had for some time, but I had never been able to get off the ground. The idea was to take the Pathé news library, which in strength dated back to 1905 (we had some shots from the 1890s). I wanted to utilize this library to make short subjects, and this was a period when this was not really done. Since then, with television, we've had a lot of so-called library compilations, but this was quite a new thing then. He listened to me, and he said he'd think it over, and sometime later I was called in and told to go ahead and produce these shorts.

"This was a dream come true, so I continued doing my regular job writing newsreel scripts, and on the side, started delving through this great library and making shorts from it."

When asked whether he enjoyed working on newsreels, Youngson responded, "Oh yes, it was tremendously interesting, a very vibrant, vital thing, and the years I was working on the newsreels were sort of the height of the newsreel. The newsreels are all gone now, because television has taken their place. Actually, the newsreels aren't gone; there is TV, which is a much degraded form. To digress for a moment, the reason I say this is that our news today consists of seeing a newscaster for about 60% or more of the time on the air, and then getting film clips. Of course the old film newsreels weren't that way; you had an off-screen narration, but your actual news pictures were the things that counted."

Youngson answered questions about the newsreels, noting they came out twice a week and have time limits that were "very very, tight limits, during the war especially. What would happen was that you would make up a whole newsreel, and then suddenly a big story would break, and the film would come in from the Signal Corps, let's say, of a great battle. You would junk all the work you had done and start from scratch, work all through the night and get the newsreel. This was common practice."

FFM asked Youngson, "If a news story broke on a Monday, how soon would you be able to have it in your newsreel?" Youngson: "Well, we were remarkably fast – of course, not as fast as television. The make-up days were Monday and Thursday. We would make up on Monday, and if the film got to the laboratory on time, in the wee hours of Tuesday morning, prints would start getting into first-run theaters on Tuesday."

As for the shorts made from the old Pathé footage, Youngson explained: "They were made entirely from old footage; on a couple of them like *World of Kids* there was some original shooting that I did, but very little. These shorts, I'm happy to say, won two Academy Awards and six nominations. They were tremendously successful, and just a delight to work on. I would decide a subject, and then go through great masses of film, screen hundreds of thousands of feet of film, and eventually emerge with that subject. It was a delightful personal enterprise; it was perhaps in the motion picture industry a rare opportunity to be creative on your own. Under this set-up, there was nobody looking over my shoulder, nobody telling me what to do. The only restrictions were certain footage restrictions, whether it would be a one-reeler or two-reeler."

Besides using old newsreel footage to make shorts, Youngson dabbled with using old movie material; *Magic Movie Moments* is his first film of that sort. Youngson: "I made a one-reel short out of *Noah's Ark* and then later I did a reissue feature version utilizing an edited version of *Noah's Ark* from 1929. The spectacle was just marvelous, and it was completed just as talkies came into prominence, and just at that precise time, the interest of the public was entirely in talkies, so they cut down the spectacle of *Noah's Ark* to a tremendous extent and added talkie sequences, which were horrible. They were saying practically nothing, but they were talking; that was in that era in order for a film to succeed. When I made my revised *Noah's Ark* as a feature I took all those sequences out; they just had no value at all, whereas the spectacle, I thought, had held up extremely well."

As regards other shorts made from movie material, Youngson noted, "*Thrills from the Past* was from an old Warner film called *Old San Francisco*, which had the San Francisco earthquake as the highlight, and *A Bit of the Best* was a condensation of Rin-Tin-Tin in a film called *Trapped by the Police.*"

FFM asked, "What were your impressions of the Warners film library? Youngson answered: "Well, I had complete access, but unfortunately, silent films mainly didn't exist; many of them were just gone. There was a period of time in which there was a feeling that silent films had no commercial value whatsoever. If I may be immodest, I think I had more to do with disproving that than anyone else. It was heartbreaking, there were so many films I wanted to get from the Warner library which had completely been destroyed. The storage of nitrate negatives is a very expensive thing, and as I rather imagined in my mind's eye, the way it occurred.

"I suppose someone came in and said, 'We have to build some new vaults.' Someone else said, 'Well, how much will it cost?' 'It will cost $500,000.' 'What's filling up your vaults now?' They looked down the list and said, 'Here's this vault filled with old silent negatives – what have they brought in the past 10 years? Nothing! Throw them out; we'll save thousands of dollars.' And so much of the history of the silent era is just gone. Basically,, the ones that were available were mainly silent films made at the end of the silent era. At the end of the silent era they added synchronized scores, and these were kept, I suppose, because they figured there was a soundtrack attached to them. All the earlier stuff was gone.

"Now that I think of it, I did utilize another talkie film, however used in silent form, and that was *An Adventure to Remember*, which was made from a very early talkie called *Isle of Lost Ships* – this was the second making of *Isle of Lost Ships*, not the Maurice Tourneur version, but one directed by Irving Willat, and it was quite an oddity among early talkie films in that it was an action film.

"During that early talkie period everything consisted of people just standing around and talking. Of course, *When the Talkies Were Young* had an appeal, I think, when it was made that isn't anywhere as great now. When I made *When the Talkies Were Young* the major companies hadn't released their old films to television, so that people who saw this short were seeing James Cagney, Edward G. Robinson, Barbara Stanwyck, Clark Gable, Spencer Tracy – they were seeing all these movie personalities whom they were seeing constantly in new films, and not realizing how they were changing through the years. All of a sudden here was this short with these people all young. It came as a tremendous shock to audiences; and it was great fun to make. Now, of course, that shock effect is gone because on TV you have so many early films."

Youngson told how he decided which sequences to put in *When the Talkies Were Young*: "It was a case where I had hoped to make ten shorts, or twenty or thirty, just like this. It was a tremendous job of selection. What I was trying to do –my main motive—was to show stars at their very beginnings, for example James Cagney in *Sinner's Holiday* with Joan Blondell. It was their first film, in both cases.

"I had already completed a second film, a sequel to *When the Talkies Were Young*, and just as I was completing it, Warner Brothers sold their entire backlog to Associated Artists, and I just dropped the whole project… the film no longer belonged to Warner Brothers. One little item that comes to mind (that I included) was Lee Tracy in *Blessed Event*, in which there was a marvelous fast-talking sequence."

As regards *50 Years Before Your Eyes*, his first feature, *FFM* asked: "Was it an outgrowth of the shorts?" Youngson: "Yes, I was the director on that, I wasn't the producer. We had come to the 50-year mark, and I had written reports urging that this film be made. I was finally allowed to make it, but I didn't have the freedom making this that I had with my other films. I was dissatisfied with it; much footage that I wanted to include couldn't be left in because a lot of footage that I thought ponderous and heavy I was forced to include.

"I don't think it's a bad film, I'm not ashamed of the film, but it's a film that I think could have been much better. In fact, I felt so strongly about my dissatisfaction with the film that I began a series [of shorts] that did the same job the way I wanted to do it. That series started with *I Remember When*, which covered material from before the turn of the century. That was followed up with *This Was Yesterday*, which took the period from the 20th century up until the outbreak of World War 1. And there was marvelous footage of the campaign of Pancho Villa in Mexico. I've always considered the newsreel footage that was made on that Mexican expedition, which mind you was made in 1915, so indicative of how far advanced we were in newsreel making. Some of the scenes are striking – there's a scene, for example, of the supply wagons going across the Mexican desert which I think is superior to any scene in *The Covered Wagon*.

"That film was followed by *It Happened to You*, which was a 2-reel coverage of America in World War 1, as seen from the homefront mainly. There was some battle material in it, but it was mainly a homefront film. And that was as far as I got, unfortunately."

FFM asked, "Why did you stop making shorts." Youngson: "Well basically, because the shorts market was shot, there wasn't any money in it anymore… not for me, so much, because I would have gone on making them forever, but as far as Warners was concerned. They had a drastic cutting-down of shorts production. Then Warner-Pathé went out of existence. And I turned to making independent features."

3

Enter Jeanne and Al

"We fell into a pleasant relationship and I'd have to say after his weight got to a certain point, he wasn't interested – wasn't able – or maybe just had to make a choice between eating to being a husband? He loved those big dinners…"

– Jeanne Keyes Youngson, 2015
Interview with Jim Manago

SOME DETAILS ABOUT YOUNGSON'S private life and the production of his compilations received attention in Scott MacGillivray's *Laurel & Hardy: From the Forties Forward* (Vestal Press, 1998). In addition, Jeanne answered my questions in 2015, including information on how she met Bob and their life together.

By the time he got married in 1960, Youngson had already made two of his eight compilations.

Jeanne: "First off when we met, he had pure white hair. Bob was impressed by his and my mutual love of films and I think that was one of the several reasons he took to me. And this is how it happened: I'd become friends with Bill Everson and the rest of the FOOFS (Friends of Old Films)…. FOOFS was the nickname for the Society, or so I've always assumed. And went to his movie showings in a building on 5th Avenue, near 14th Street. At the time I had a glamour job as a receptionist at MCA as the MoMA had that awful fire in 1958.

"Everson screened Bob's *This Mechanical Age* that night and introduced me to Bob who was also there. A heavy-set, very handsome fellow with prematurely white hair he was, and he lit up the minute we met. Working at MCA, I'd been associating with gorgeous actors and dishy agents and thought, well, he seems like a nice guy and I love his movie… but that was it. He asked me out for coffee… coffee? At 10-o-clock at night? Not on your tintype."

Jeanne told MacGillivray regarding a film screening at MoMA: "One night I saw this very handsome fellow in there, but he was kind of overweight, which didn't appeal to me."

Jeanne to Manago: [Bob was] a lovely man, really a lovely person. He was real old-world, courtly fellow.

"He asked me out three more times and I kept saying no. One evening after work I went to see a Debbie Reynold's movie on 3rd Avenue [and 68th Street], *Gazebo*, and he was sitting in the row ahead of me. Alone. I tapped him on the shoulder, and he motioned for me to come up and sit next to him… and that was the beginning. And he finally asked me out for a DRINK! We dated for several months and one night he got down on his knees and proposed.

"The agents at MCA kept calling me a 'trophy bride' which was a terrific compliment. They kept insisting I give up the idea of getting married and move to Hollywood. Universal was taking over (absorbing?) the organization. Mimi Weber asked me to train to be an agent in her office out there but my mom wanted me to get married, and so did I.

"Bob a loner? He never mentioned having pals while growing up… Bob was a loner. He had one best friend growing up, Bernie Shapiro, who was best man at our wedding. He was very close to his parents and went to see them several times a week in Brooklyn. The four of us also went to Atlantic City on weekends.

"They remained friends until Bob's death, and after that Bernie kind of faded away because our lives took different directions, I guess. Bernie's dad was in the wedding dress business on 7th Avenue, and a gown was Bernie's wedding gift to us. Mom came down to New York from Sussex, N.J. and we went to see what was available. They chose a nice dress for me (my fave was much less expensive!) We were to be wed in the bay window in my parents' house in Sussex.

"There were 75 people invited including Bob's mom and dad, my uncle and aunt from Pennsylvania, people I worked with at MCA and friends of the family in Sussex. Bob invited about seven couples, older men he worked with in the city and their wives, none of which (my mother noted) gave us gifts. I didn't know any of them. Bernie was his only friend present.

"After the wedding, my uncle Charles (a physician) told my parents that Bob 'wouldn't last more than seven years!' He beat those odds.

"Uncle Charles took one look at Bob and that was that. Bob was heavy, yes, but one forgot about it as soon as he turned on that charm."

"I have a much younger brother & sister and they both thought Bob was OK. Their dad was my stepfather."

Jeanne, born on December 20, 1924, as Margaret Jeanne Keyes, 38, married Robert George Youngson, 42, on June 25, 1960.

Jeanne: "Why did I marry Bob? After we'd met, I was taken aside by Bill Everson who told me Bob was rich and a good catch. I actually did not know he had money. He didn't flaunt it and as far as I could tell, he only spent $$$ on dining out. He was really handsome and charming.

"Once he began courting, there was no stopping him. He asked dad for my hand, and even went to Sussex to tell Mom he wanted us to elope, as he didn't want to wait a whole month to get married. Poor Mom & little sister sent out invitations and got the affair, including a reception for 75, ready in just two weeks! I'm not telling you this to self-aggrandize, but to show [you] that once he made up his mind, he was a powerhouse of… intent? And he may have sensed that I was a permanent 'fixture?' Does that make sense?

"Well, I'll tell you. I had had boyfriends before but never did one seem to adore me as much as Bob did. Sounds self-serving, but it wasn't long before he wanted to marry me, (3 months) even got on his knees to propose AND asked my dad, too. (Like in old movies.) He hadn't been serious with anyone until he was 42 years old. In fact, his mom (in front of my sister, although she didn't realize it) told people at the reception: 'I guess she's pregnant and that's why they have to get married. He's too young!' Imagine!

"Bob's mother died six months after we got married. She was never friendly and as I guess I told you, she just didn't want Bob to get married. He loved weekends in Atlantic City, though, so I went along. It would have been September 1960 that we took the [Washington Square] penthouse. Robert Whitehead & wife were living here but she had cancer. I don't know the story. I met her a couple of times about the terrace boxes which we bought (from her) as I loved to garden. Whitehead's wife died of cancer not too long after they moved to Lincoln Center. He later married Zoe Caldwell, I believe.

[Before I got married,] Mimi Weber asked me to go to California and that she would train me to be an agent. This was 1959 when Universal was taking over MCA or whatever was going on with that whole deal. My mom didn't want me to go to California and said she would feel better if I was closer – and married.

My questions about Bob meant Jeanne would think back of the many fine things from over fifty-five years ago. Jeanne: "You got me musing about our marriage which started a train of thought about the pre-days. If his former girlfriend looked like Gene Tierney and he was interested in beauty, why didn't he marry her? My dad was a doctor (veterinarian) and we had a lovely home in the suburbs. I think Bob was impressed by my lineage, my love of movies, and my sense of humor. The fact that I had inherited money from my grandmother didn't hurt either.

I asked Jeanne, 'You didn't see yourself as beautiful or attractive to Bob? Was Bob the romantic type with you?" Jeanne responded by offering "charm" as one of Bob's strongest points. Jeanne: "His strongest point? His work and he could charm the boids outta the treeze – if he needed or wanted to. He didn't seem to have any other interests besides movies. I know he did have girlfriends before I met him."

About fifteen years ago, Jeanne had told MacGillivray: "One time he said, 'I'm not really interested in anything but film.' No hobbies, except going to the movies, that's what we shared. And that was it."

Jeanne reiterated this to me: "Beauty? He told me he had been dating a gal who looked like Tierney and she was with him when he got the Oscar. I suppose I was cute rather than classic. He must have liked my looks. I had been dating Greg Garrison and other luminaries I met at MCA, even had a few dates with Larry Tierney. Bob was absolutely gaga when we met. And I turned down two dates with him before that night at the movies. He had asked me to go out for coffee! Imagine. 10 pm. When he offered 'a drink'... YAY!... New ballgame. He was romantic, yes. I really don't know what to say about that.

"We fell into a pleasant relationship and I'd have to say after his weight got to a certain point, he wasn't interested – wasn't able – or maybe just had to make a choice between eating to being a husband? He loved those big dinners...

"We had two apartments in the Village, and [now 55 years later] I am still in the penthouse. When he died, I gave up the suite at #1 Fifth Avenue and moved to a smaller one (there) where I had a Dracula Museum; and held Count Dracula Fan Club meetings. The club now is The Vampire Empire/

Bram Stoker Memorial Association, and this year we are celebrating our Golden Anniversary. Bob loved the tie-in with horror movies.

"So he had been living in a hotel up on 49th Street just off Madison and working there. It was the New Weston Hotel where we lived at first, 50th & Madison. Bob kept the New Weston office/apartment for some time, along with the apartment/office on 5th Avenue.

"I remember him interviewing Bob & Ray (radio personalities) and E.G. Marshall as possible commentators/voice-overs on the movie he was working on in 1961 (in the office uptown). And it was in the New Weston that my 3 1/2 carat diamond engagement ring was stolen in 1961, so we were still spending nights there now and then.

"I was thinking last night about my engagement ring. His dad had given a jeweler on Canal Street a huge discount on a used car, so when we got engaged, we went down to this guy's place and I chose the ring which Bob got for a pittance.

"After the wedding and engagement rings were stolen, they were not replaced. I finally went to Gimbles and bought another set, which I still have. [After Bob died, I did not remarry.]

"Al would come in every day to do his bidding. There were wonderful places to dine in the area, and his modus operandi was to take it easy during the day food-wise and then at night to have a huge meal. We moved to the Village in September (1960), to the penthouse where I still am, and in January (1961) he got the apartment at #1 Fifth Avenue and moved his stuff out of the hotel.

Everson told MacGillivray: "He was *always* here in New York. He had a very big apartment at 1 Fifth Avenue, and he and Jeanne lived just across the square in a penthouse. But almost all the work was done at 1 Fifth Avenue. I sat in on a lot of screenings there, and Al Dahlem, his cutter, would work out of there."

Bob had some unexpressed but serious issues concerning money and his marriage that even Jeanne could not resolve them. Jeanne: "I think he had a problem with money as, after we were married, he refused to open a joint bank account. This worried my dad; as well, it might for after he died… well, I'll come to that later. He gave me an allowance for utilities and rent at the penthouse, and a bit besides. As time went by, we spent more and more time in the suite on 5th Avenue.

"Regarding money and Bob, I never had an inkling of how much he got or had. I had money of my own so did not push it. He spent on those dinners, rent, gosh, don't really know what else. He lived first class all the way.

"His sister was always griping about how I was younger than she was. I wasn't close to her or her family, but we were pleasant. Don't know when any of them died, except Bob's mom who died in December 1960. (I wasn't even 50 when Bob died.)

"Back to the money business, my parents (everyone) knew Bob had substantial funds and did not like the fact that I was having to spend my own money after we were married. Mom urged me to get him to a marriage counselor and I finally talked him into going to Albert Ellis. Once we got there and he found out why, he walked out. He did raise my allowance very slightly, but only a few dollars.

As far as having children, Jeanne revealed, "Of course the fact that we both loved movies played a part and being basically loners came into play. Sure, kids would have come BUT I had to go on birth control pills right after we were married, due to endometriosis. Talk about pain. Yeow!"

One of Bob's child-like curiosities was his fascination with Christmas. Jeanne: "Bob loved Christmas. I collected gifts all year long and there would be piles and piles of them under the tree. It would take him all Christmas afternoon to open them all. I also gave him one fabulous gift, usually an antique: A real W.C. Field's barber chair, a merry-go-round horse from the Coney Island fire, a giant RCA Victor dog, for example. "[I] still have pictures of these although the dog went to Vienna with the Dracula Museum collection (his name was "Nipper" & he later became the club mascot).

"Bob would have Al (Dahlem) go out and get me something, but Christmas was HIS day and he made the most [of it]."

Exactly when Bob met up with Al, what one could call "Bob's Man Friday" is unknown. It seemed that Al's association with Bob came at some point after Bob started doing the Warner-Pathé shorts in 1948. What happened to Youngson was that after WWII, he had returned to the studio. There he wrote and produced short subjects that he compiled from their newsreel library and from early silent and "primitive" sound films.

Jeanne: "I still don't know how much Al contributed to making the films." Jeanne had the impression that Al had little to do with the actual compilations. Jeanne said, "No, Al did not go West with Bob that I ever knew. Maybe before we met?" However, Everson credited him in film program notes as "Bob's editor and librarian." Nevertheless, Al is credited on Bob's compilations early on as "Assistant Producer, Al Dahlem."

Others credited on Bob's compilations included his nephew, Richard Tonini and Bob's dad, I. Hill Youngson. Jeanne: "Richard was just a young kid and Dad (I. Hill Youngson) was Dad. I know Bob worked day and night on them so it's possible he did them alone." With other names mentioned, Jeanne had no memory; for instance as for Kogan, Jeanne: "He doesn't ring a bell. Jack Shaindlin [musical score for *Days of Thrills and Laughter*], nice fellow. Herb Gelbspan was a wonderful guy. He sent me Christmas cards for years." [Gelbspan represented Hal Roach Studios in New York].

"It occurs to me that the only people alive today that knew Bob Youngson would be me and his nephew and niece in California who were small children when we went out to see his sister. The rest of his family is gone."

As far as Al, Jeanne noted, "I can't tell you much about Al. He had worked with him at Pathé, and when Bob left, he hired him to become his… sort of assistant & gofer. Al's long gone, of course. He was a big sort of teddy bear fellow. They lived in Queens or at least out in that direction. They had two children. The boy died – gosh, so long ago I don't remember from what. I seem to recall the daughter got married a couple of times, and they moved down to, I don't know? Some southern state to be near her. But Al had a health/respiratory problem and was not a well person. Maybe I'll think of what it was.

"I doubt Bob ever set foot in a department store. Being a person who delegated, it was natural for him to have Al run his errands. Al as editor? Don't know how much editing he did. They did not work while I was present. During the week they had the day to do film stuff and on weekends Bob and I had people in (to #1 5th Avenue) to see movies. He had two 16mm projectors.

"If I was busy elsewhere on Saturday, he had a couple of regular film mavens in to see movies and keep him company. Don Miller and Ed Connor, mainly. Weekend guests were people I knew… Ed Gorey – always brought a gift or one of his books.

"Bob was 96% occupied with movies, especially old ones. Well, loving old films, he would have seen *Nosferatu*, etc., right? And when I founded the Count Dracula Fan Club in 1965, he let his Man Friday Al Dahlem help whenever I needed it.

"I guess he learned about film making while working at Pathé. He did go to the west coast a lot, working through the 1960s on all those films. He slowed down after [his last silent film compilation], *4 Clowns*, and then quite a bit in the early 1970s although he said he was working on something but didn't say what.

"He went to Hollywood quite often. I'd been there under different circumstances before we met and at first he asked me to go with him. This meant I had to wait in a motel or hotel while he worked at the studios, which was boring and dull and after two times, I said that was it."

Jeanne told MacGillivray: "Later on, when he started working at M-G-M and Fox, he was going out to the west coast quite frequently. He took me out there a few times to sightsee a few thousand times," she laughs. In addition, "I'm sure it was a couple of years for each one [each compilation], because it was blood, sweat, and tears. Nothing was easy, it seemed. He was so painstaking when he made his movies, [but] he seemed to be perpetually in a cloud while he was working."

In 1970, after his final compilation *4 Clowns* was released, Jeanne said to MacGillivray, "I know there were some guys that handled their own stuff, and they wouldn't let him have it. Harold Lloyd, for example. I think Robert was very disappointed about that, even though we were great friends with Harold Lloyd. When Robert was gung-ho about moving to California, he wanted to buy Harold Lloyd's house."

Jeanne: "In those days he and Al would go driving (in Al's car) in the country and they'd have those huge lunches. In the early evening, I'd go over to the apartment and he'd send Al downstairs to get me a meal from one of the local restaurants. Re-reading this, it sounds like a weird arrangement but that's the way it was."

There was another characteristic to Bob. It became obvious to anyone who knew him. It really factored in his success at reviving interest among the public in silent comedies. It had nothing to do at all with his obsessive love of the films and that era. Perhaps most important is that Bob had an all-consuming and strong work ethic. Though he succeeded in obscuring his flaws this way, it allowed him to be capable of some truly fine achievements when given half a chance.

Jeanne: "Yes, Bob was a worker and loved what he did. He worked day and night. He would sit and chew a handkerchief and I'd find tattered hankies around the place. He sometimes worked late, and then spent the night over there."

Earlier and similarly, Jeanne told MacGillivray: "He got a little nervous in between, before he started another project. His thing was biting handkerchiefs while he worked – and boy, we had a lot of shredded handkerchiefs around our house!"

4

Film, Food and Friends

"As I said, Bob had to have first class all the way. I guess having his parents spoil him to the extent they did made him the way he was, talented for sure, charming and charismatic but lacking a certain sensitivity? chip, as the former Mrs. Brad Pitt put it."

– Jeanne Keyes Youngson,
Interview with Jim Manago

HOW BOB SINGLE-HANDEDLY revived interest in silent film comedies, especially Laurel and Hardy, had partly to do with his immense interest that he nurtured. Over the years, he watched many films with various friends at his apartment or theirs. Most notable is the film viewing he did with associates, such as William K. Everson, who was already at the time a well-known film authority and film collector. Bill showed films from his own collection in his Upper West Side New York City apartment.

The practices of a number of individuals involved in a developing East Coast film culture are detailed in an interview of producer/director Charles L. Turner conducted by Museum of Modern Art's Ronald S. Magliozzi ("Witnessing the Development of Independent Film Culture in New York: An Interview with Charles L. Turner).

Magliozzi and Turner's comments are useful in understanding Youngson's practice of showing films in private or semi-public settings with other interested professionals associated with the film business and art. This is at a time before television or theaters would show old movies regularly.

From the beginning, there were those individuals who started societies or clubs. For example, radio actor John Griggs ran the "Sutton Cinema Society," named for the location of his apartment on Sutton Place where he screened the films he collected. Magliozzi: "His audiences were largely people in the Arts, mostly actors and writers. He ran a lot of films at The Players Club. He had Lilian Gish, Vivien Leigh, Anthony Perkins and others to see the films at his home through the years. To add to the events, he even played the piano with the silent pictures."

Youngson's involvement or awareness of Griggs' group is unknown. However, his involvement in the burgeoning film culture seemed to be with a community group called "The Film Circle." The invitees and regulars met in New York City beginning in early 1952. Among the regulars were producer Richard Gordon, the film dealer/collector John E. Allen, Everson, etc.

Magliozzi: "Turner kept notes on 'The Film Circle' which contain the following list of individuals invited to the first meeting: 'John E. Allen, film dealer and collector, Mary Ellen Bute, filmmaker; Elspeth Chapin (secretary for *Films in Review*); Woodrow Gelman; Henry Hart, editor of *Films in Review*; William Kenly (later Paramount Pictures publicist), Steven Lewis; Gerald McDonald, NYPL film stills archivist; Louis A. McMahon, cameraman; Ted Nemeth, cameraman and producer; Joseph Noble, partner in Film Counselors; Mark Sandrich, Jr.; Richard Taylor; Parker Tyler; Amos Vogel; Chuck Wasserman, director; Herman Weinberg; Robert Youngson, filmmaker.' After the first two programmes had been run, the following names were added: 'George Geltzer, collector; James Gregory, actor; John Griggs, actor and collector; Perry Miller; Stanley Russell; Seymour Stern, D.W. Griffith enthusiast and biographer.' It is important to note that this is a list of the first invited members and not a record of all those who attended."

Turner explained in detail of how "The Film Circle," began meeting, at first, at least once every two weeks at Film Counselors, 500 Fifth Avenue near 42nd Street in New York City. They "had a projection room because a lot of their work was screening films for clients. They acted as go-betweens or overseers for an industry or a company who wanted to commission films but who didn't know anything about filmmaking."

Weinberg seemed to be the only one who did not like the name of "The Film Circle," apparently saying, it "Sounds like a sewing circle!" After Theodore (Ted) Huff died of an internal hemorrhage in March of 1953, the name of the group was changed. In memory of Ted, it was renamed the "Theodore Huff Memorial Film Society." Everson took over the group and single-handedly ran it, perhaps as early as October 1953.

Under Everson's management, the film screenings of the Theodore Huff Memorial Film Society continued to run regularly. One report said the group met at the Radio Writers Guild headquarters at 2 East 23rd Street in New York City. Everson, Weinberg, and Warren Rosenberger were credited with writing the program (or as some prefer, programme) notes, while Youngson served as the Program Secretary and Turner as the Chairman of the Society. The group would have discussions afterwards eating at The Brass Rail.

In the society's first year, Turner kept a written record of the films that were shown. In Programme #7, on May 2, 1952, among the films screened was an unnamed "Newsreel by Bob Youngson."

It is clear what Turner did best besides making films for business, military and personal projects, is that he participated in such film activities. Youngson did likewise. Magliozzi noted that Turner: "… became involved in an informal community of film professionals, journalists, film buffs and historians whose interaction served to influence the climate, the resources and the method of film study…. Their activities developed as an expression of undisciplined affection for the cinema, and took four related forms: collection of film and memorabilia; exhibition of film at alternative, private and semi-public sites; writing of historical texts, largely in the form of programme notes, periodical writing and letters; and oral communication through unstructured gatherings and gossip."

It is certain that Youngson participated in contributing to a developing East Coast film culture in at least three of these four ways. Indeed, he collected films. He also exhibited films as described, and he communicated orally as he attended various screenings organized by him, and others. What is uncertain is whether Youngson regularly wrote program notes, periodical articles or letters; and it is unknown if he did some of these things, even for a short time.

In another footnote to the Magliozzi and Turner article taken from interviews with William Kenly, Youngson reportedly had some problems with the latter at the film screenings. Kenly's employment is described "from the 1950s through the 1960s [as] cinema manager in New York at 5th Avenue Playhouse, The Paris, Cinema Village, Grove Press theatre, and The World (Philadelphia); music librarian at Channel 13 (NY), then publicist and 'unofficial archivist' with Paramount Pictures, 1968-1991."

As regards the relationship between Kenly and Youngson, Magliozzi noted, "Huff's death and Turner's absence from the organization left (Bill) Kenly in charge of its screening activities, 'moving from one spot to another screening films… dragging the projectors… doing the scores, writing the notes.' Everson was helpful through this period, allowing Kenly to pre-screen films at the Monogram Studio offices where Everson was then working, and allowing Kenly with access to Monogram's mimeograph machine for printing program notes.

"Meanwhile, Kenly's friendship with Huff Society member Robert Youngson was failing. Kenly states that although Youngson 'attended screenings religiously,' he made no effort to work on behalf of the organization and was 'inclined to be a complainer.' A falling out between them triggered by the release of *The Robe* at the Roxy Theatre in September 1953, lead to Kenly's resigning his Huff Society duties."

Jeanne: "I'm surprised at the Kenly business. I knew him at MoMA and he was always pleasant. As for Bob, he'd go to a movie wherever it was. He was a fanatic about work. As I told you, he used to work late at night in the apartment at #1 Fifth Avenue so I can't imagine him having time to… do what for the Huffs? What did they want him to do?

"Surely there's more to the story… he wasn't the kind of guy to 'hang out' with other (non-productive) film buffs so… well, who knows? Anyway, as far as I am aware, Kenly was just another of the regular gang. I didn't know about the rest of the stuff, bottom line being that Bob never mentioned Kenly and was best pals with Bill Everson until he died. Thinking back: the people he showed movies to, usually afternoons when I was busy and Al was off included Bill Everson, Ed Connor, Ed Gorey, and Don Miller."

Besides some issue with Kenly, it is clear that Youngson seemed to have some other falling out or something with at least one other individual, James Card. This is evident from Card's remarks in his book after Youngson's death that reveals some repulsion that developed concerning Youngson. Jeanne explained: "Bob had a friend, Jim Card, who was the head of the Eastman House Film Collection (something like that). We'd go up to Rochester for weekend festivals. I remember Gloria Swanson being at one and griping about the hotel-motel we were in – 'The Threadbare Inn.' Ha! Ha!

"[At] another time Jim Card brought Louise Brooks down and I guess they stayed here in the penthouse… Not sure about how that worked out, but was I ever shocked at what that former beauty looked like, with greying hair and bad teeth and she was very shy – or maybe withdrawn. But you know that whole story.

"I don't know what happened between Bob and Jim. Maybe nothing. STILL, I was shocked to read what Jim said in some book or other about Bob's condition near the end of his life. "Gross, unable to walk, etc." True, he was very heavy but was still able to walk down the street."

I located the actual remark that upset Jeanne. It came from Card's 1997 book, *Seductive Cinema: The Art of the Silent Films*. Card closed his reference to Bob saying, "Later Bob would work for MGM and, at more than six hundred pounds, grow too unwieldy to leave his prestigious #1 Fifth Avenue address."

When I relayed the actual quote to Jeanne, she was truly shocked. Jeanne: "Wow! 600 pounds. Never. Inconceivable. As I said, he was able to walk a block at least – until he died, I can only guess there had been some kind of, I don't know – disagreement? – between him and Card, but I thought they were friends. Card used to stay in Bob's apartment/office or here in the penthouse when he came down from Rochester. He always had stories about Louise Brooks… one was that when he and she were screening her movies at Eastman House, she said to him, 'You only like who I was.'

"As for the weight, I do not think Bob could help himself. It was such a pleasure for him to eat. Funny that his dad, who loved him so much, would actually take him to famous places in Brooklyn, and they would eat meals for hours. His father did not gain weight and you'd think he might have discouraged his son to maybe take it easy? Another mystery."

Jeanne thought of a pertinent question: "Do you suppose that since Mom and Dad never denied him anything and treated him like a god, he didn't deny himself food? In retrospect, it would seem irrational that he would let himself go like that… .

"His weight? I'd guess the highest would have been about 450 and the lowest 250 pounds. He neglected his health insofar as food intake was concerned and seemed not to be aware of being heavy. [Back in 1952 long before I met him], do you think that might subconsciously have been the reason he shunned publicity and didn't go to the Oscars for *World of Kids*? I never thought of that before."

However, Youngson did appear onstage to accept his second Academy Award.

Maltin noted, "Bob was obese. I couldn't hazard a guess as to his weight."

Jeanne added, "He worked steadily through the '60s on *Days of Thrills and Laughter*, *The Big Parade of Comedy*, *Laurel and Hardy's Laughing 20s*, *Further Perils of Laurel and Hardy*, *4 Clowns*. And although I had taken a course in cooking in Florence, he didn't care to break up the day by coming over here for dinner, then going back to work. (And he did LOVE to eat out!)"

The newspapers later reported that Bob had spent much time watching films with Card, Eastman House's curator in Rochester, New York. Card had a penchant for insisting on enjoying the original, but quite flammable nitrate films from his very large personal collection. He used to say he preferred them, as he loved the smell of the nitrates.

Card revealed one particular remembrance of Youngson at those screenings. In fact, Card's insistence on continuing to preserve the nitrate films instead of transferring them to safety film put him at odds with other institutions that long abandoned holding nitrate originals.

Card: "The Moviegraph had been replaced by a Holmes Portable, madly set up right next to the coal-burning furnace. Often the projectionist was John Allen, coolly running the nitrate while puffing on a pipe that gave off smoke and sparks like a locomotive on a mountain upgrade. After several years of living this dangerously, the projector was donated to Eastman House, and the screening room moved up to the attic.

"That third-floor retreat became a mecca for film people from Chicago, Manhattan, Berlin and Paris. Bob Youngson was among them when he only weighed 350, stomping the floor so that the walls trembled in his unrestrained hilarity as he watched some rare comedy. Bob gained great success editing extant footage into shorts and features for Warner Brothers. One of those two-reelers brought him an Academy Award." (Of course, Card missed the fact that Bob actually won two Academy Awards).

Jeanne: "It always sounded like he got along great with West Coast studio people and the guy who did his music here. You have his name, I'm sure. Jack?" That was Jack Shaindlin.

"Bob did not smoke, drink or take drugs. [He] didn't like being around people who smoked – [but he] always let me have my vodka martinis.

"Bob's favorite food? Anything, but he did love the big pretzels on the street and after our Sunday afternoon movie uptown, always got one or two to eat at home.

"Favorite movies? Anything and everything. I don't remember him reading books. He liked *All in the Family*, and as he didn't like to go out at night we watched TV, or he would show a movie from his collection.

He bought a special collection of early B&W silent shorts from Jim Card which I loved to see."

If one were to briefly describe Bob's physical and personality traits, Jeanne summed it up by saying: "He was about 5'10", always wore a suit and bow tie – never anything casual – and his voice was a normal masculine voice. His voice was very pleasant, non-descript. Bob, was, as you already know, a fairly one-dimensional person.

Concerning his personality, Jeanne explained, "I could qualify a couple of items… 1). INDEPENDENT: Well, I guess he was independent insofar as his work was concerned. However, he needed a warm body near him at all times. When he went to the West Coast and I was free to travel, I had to make sure I was home when he got back.

"Al was with him during the day, I was with him every evening. He had Don Miller and Ed Connor in to watch movies with him on Saturday afternoons, and Bill Everson would occasionally come to screen films. I also was involved with Everson – I have those photos – when he was researching horror films. My collection of horror memorabilia (which eventually became the Dracula Museum) thrilled him. He gave me a copy of his horror book with the inscription, 'With admiration and affection.' Nice, eh?

"2). CONFIDENT: About his films.

"3). INTELLIGENT: Likewise.

"4). EGOCENTRIC: Thanks to Mom & Dad."

Everson told MacGillivray: "He loved to get opinions, but he would never really accept them if they disagreed with his own. If he thought something was great and it *was* great, everybody else agreed and he was delighted to have it confirmed. But if other people disagreed with him, he felt they were wrong, and he would just go his own way. Which was his privilege."

Jeanne: "Yes, Bob laughed at the old comedies. He did have a hearty laugh. No sound recordings that I know of. He did laugh at his own movies. Don't remember him laughing at [new] comedies, i.e. Woody Allen stuff. I think they amused him but I'd say he was 'tuned in' to oldies.

"His sleeping habits… when he stayed at the penthouse with me, he got up and down when I did… 8 a.m. to 11 p.m. When he stayed at #1 Fifth, I think he worked late."

Some have questioned where Bob got his own collection of films that he showed to friends and associates over the years, and if they had anything to do with his film compilations. Well, the question brings up the matter of an uncle that Jeanne never heard Bob ever mentioning.

Brent Walker's study of Youngson's sources for his compilations offered a possible answer to the question of where Youngson got his personal collection of films. Walker: "Youngson possessed a large film collection that, according to film historian and author Ed Watz, included a great number of 35mm silents that he had inherited from his uncle Erich Shea, a former Goldwyn executive who had passed away in the thirties."

Watz confirmed that his information came from one of Youngson's Brooklyn, New York cousins; namely, Barbara Grattan. Watz: "Barbara's father was an employee of Sam Goldwyn… He died in 1933 so I can't imagine any film acquisitions after that date. But Barbara recalled Robert coming to their house all the time as a kid. … She was an Executive Administrator of the Brooklyn Union Gas Company sometime in the 1980s.

"The last contact I had with Barbara was when she retired. I do know that she lived in Bay Ridge, Brooklyn and I did see her on the street there around 1995. My guess is that if she is alive [today in 2015], she would be at least 90 years old.

"Barbara had told me that Bob needed someone like Jeanne around because she basically had to buy clothes for him, etcetera. Perhaps there's a family animosity at work here, who knows?"

However, Jeanne responded that she knew for sure that Bob did not have a collection of 35mm films. He had 16mm films galore and projectors for those films – but no 35mms. She questioned the validity of this account which is supposedly a claim attributed to Barbara.

Jeanne: "An inheritance from an Erich Shea? Wow. Never heard that before. COMPLETE SURPRISE! Exec at Goldwyn/MGM? Where'd that come from? I would certainly have known something about an inheritance or personal connection with Goldwyn. I doubt this 100%. He certainly would have told me about a relative at Goldwyn. He built up his collection of films once we had room here in the Village. What he brought down here were the Pathé newsreels and a FEW full-length feature films.

"A great number of 35mm silents? No way. And from an uncle he never mentioned? We had two 16mm projectors, one here at the penthouse & one at #1 Fifth Avenue on which he showed the movies he had. Someone is mistaken.

"Yes, he had a cousin (Barbara Grattan) in Brooklyn that kept calling and calling – both of us, in fact. He kept putting her off. I don't know if she was a first cousin or what. It was over 50 years ago, but I do remember he had no interest in meeting with her. He never mentioned a connection with Goldwyn, which is strange, especially if he had a relative there who might have pulled some strings. Not that his movies needed strings pulled…

"Probably Bob (and Bernie) spent time at Barbara's house as they seemed to have been BFFs in spades."

Jeanne asked me, "You got in touch with her? Did she remember calling us all the time after we were married? I remember him not wanting to speak with her. Bob would have been about 16 when Barbara's father died. Anyway, he did not have a large collection of those films as per our former collection.

"I don't know about the 35mm silents you mention. I knew about Bob's film collection including the wonderful B&W shorts he bought from Jim Card, when he acquired them and how much he paid. Bob did not store his collection of movies, what he had he brought down here. And I do not recall any 35mm silents.

"We had 16mm projectors and those are what he used to screen movies for friends. If he had received films from 'Unk,' where would he have had them? There were never storage bills (later) and I saw the film cans that came down to #1 Fifth from his small place at the New Weston. He had 16mm movies, true, but I only remember a few 35mm cans. And when he died and everything was moved downstairs to my apartment (at #1 Fifth) – there were his 16mm movies and the collection of Pathé films.

"Bob seemed to have no interest in meeting Barbara. [I] hope she's still alive as I am curious as to what she would say. If there were 35mms, why didn't they ever turn up? And why wouldn't he have mentioned them? Or told me he had an uncle at MGM? Very odd.

"John E. Allen was very much in the picture. [Film dealer and film lab supervisor Allen got billed along with Dahlem as Assistant Producer starting with *When Comedy Was King*.] They did a lot of business together. There was also another guy that Bob didn't seem to like. I think his name was Robert Rohauer, something like that [Actually, his name is Raymond]. Bob didn't trust him but I think there was some interaction. I see the Rohauer stuff is now owned by the Cohen Film Collection.

"Bob did say Rohauer was out for two things: personal publicity and MONEY. I never met him but did see him being interviewed (on the screen) before a movie they showed at the Film Forum."

MacGillivray explained: "A chance meeting with Buster Keaton in 1952 led Rohauer to pursue a one-man crusade to get Keaton's old-silent films preserved and distributed. Rohauer used all manner of persuasions, threats, and maneuvers, legal and otherwise, to collect the entire Keaton library and control the rights himself. He jealously guarded his prize from his envious peers, and re-edited the silent films (with rewritten titles) to trademark his coveted property."

As regards Bob's film collection, Jeanne added, "Bob also had a collection of very early pornies, black sox stuff which he showed me once. Later Al Goldstein's partner, Jim Buckley, made a pornie and borrowed some of Bob's films for that. (Al Goldstein was my friend originally and I introduced him to Bob. I've done a piece on Goldstein which you'd get a kick out of.)

Jeanne recalled some of the many people that Bob got along with, and easily dropped many names of people, most who are no longer alive. Jeanne: "Well, Don Miller wrote for *Films in Review*, Ed Connor was a pleasant guy and always glad to spend an afternoon with Bob looking at movies; I worked with Frank O'Hara at the MoMA Front Desk and met Ed Gorey (and the whole gang) through him. Name 'em. I knew 'em. John Asbury, etc. Henry Hart, Arthur Kleiner, Card. I was close friends with Everson's first wife, Sandy. Bob and I used to go to movies at the Everson's West Side places and I knew Sandy when she was carrying both Bambi and Griffith.

"Later, when Bill married his second wife, we went to their place – still on the West Side to see movies at night. Everson was delighted with the Count Dracula Fan Club and hand-wrote a lovely note (inscription?) in the front of his horror-movie book. We were very close."

"We belonged to the National Board of Review and went to their movies one or two afternoons a week. We'd take a cab up and back. I think we rose and spoke our opinions after seeing a movie via the National Board. Mostly older people, as I recall. Henry Hart was always there."

When I asked about her own life, Jeanne brought my focus back to Bob, who she reminded me, is after all the subject of my book. However, she did reveal some interesting things.

Jeanne: "Oh yeah, I did a lot of research for him in the NYPL and got credited in his films. I didn't do research for all his movies. Anyway, I was so busy he knew I really didn't have time. I don't have any contracts or anything at all pertaining to his work. Nothing! I can only guess Al disposed of the paperwork and his daily appointment books. Bob never discussed anything financial with me and since this was a sore spot with him, I didn't push it.

"My real father was John Kenneth Francis. He and Mom were divorced shortly after I was born and she went in training to be a nurse. I lived with my grandmother until she remarried. This was upstate New York. When I was 9 years old, she married veterinarian Kenneth Keyes and they had two kids, Margie and Kenny. Baby-sitting. Yay! We lived in Sussex, New Jersey. That was where I took flying lessons when I was 16 and later taught instrument flying as a WAVE. But this isn't about me…

"HOWEVER, you'd probably be interested in how I happened to be in Gibsonton, Florida, during the winter, which is where the circus and carnival freaks spent the season… but again, this has nothing to do with Bob, so…"

"My work before Bob? I received a scholarship from the Museum of Modern Art (MoMA) to study at the NYU Graduate School of Fine Art, 'Art of the High Renaissance' in 1950. I went to the Museum for an interview with the Assistant Secretary, Allen Porter. He lived in a building next to Shirley Booth on 54th Street. He told me I had the choice of working days at the front desk and going to school at night or taking classes during the day and not working at the museum. Of course, I wanted to work there and eventually became Assistant Manager.

"After the fire in 1958 I got a job as receptionist at MCA and met Bob at the FOOFS. I worked at the MoMA for pay at first; later – as a married lady – I was a volunteer. Now I work with a group that plans programs for seniors. This is a now-and-then thing. And we get paid.

"I was on the Joe Franklin Show after Bob died but not because of him. I knew Joe's wife, Lois, who was, in fact, a nude model at the art school I attended in New Jersey. I guess they had a friendly separation as she moved to and lived in Florida for many years. I didn't see her mentioned in the Daily News obit and meant to check further but then forgot. The last time I saw Joe was at the Film Forum last year (2014). We had a lovely warm chat and he said he'd wanted me to return to the show but then there were complications on his end.

"I'd always loved movies and while working at the MoMA (the first time) had ample opportunity to see the oldies they showed. There was also a Film Library headed by Victor D'Amico who let me come in and cruise through old movie magazines and bios. But my best pal there was Arthur Kleiner, their official pianist for the silents. He sort of adopted me, introducing me to Theda Bara and Richard Barthelmess among others.

"Bob worked mostly at Fox and MGM in Hollywood… as far as I know. The situation was that I could travel wherever I wanted while he was away, as long as I was home when he got back. I never knew him to mention having an office there. He almost never spoke about his work.

"In 1970 we went to England. I'd been there often and knew it well. When he was on the West Coast, I was free to go wherever I wanted to and London was one of my favorite spots.

"As I said, Bob went to the West Coast quite often so I would usually travel while he was away. In 1965, I went to Romania with a German group, a rather spontaneous trip, as I just happened to be in Berlin. I already knew about Bram Stoker and on the trip, the guide talked about Vlad the Impaler a lot. I was fascinated and thought, if I find this interesting, others might, too.

"So when I got back to New York, I founded the Count Dracula Fan Club. It was a success and later led to the formation of the world's only Dracula Museum, which I established in the late 1980s. (You know, of course, about Forry Ackerman, one of our mentors.) Then the cost of maintenance got too high at #1 Fifth, and I knew I had to sell everything including the museum. By this time, all Bob's stuff was gone."

"The word went out and I heard from a theatre complex in Vienna, Austria, which said they wanted to buy the collection which would be in an adjunct building (?); and, on view while Roman Polanski's musical version of his vampire movie was playing. I also heard from the Smithsonian which wanted the Bram Stoker Archive but the people in Vienna wouldn't take the collection if it was not complete.

"Bob was delighted with my Dracula society and had Al help me with newsletters, post office, errands, etc. Bob thought it was a scream. (Sorry.) He was even more into the/my transsexual saga. As I said, he was the one who suggested I do a documentary about Debbie Hartin (originally Austin Vincent Hartin) and coincidentally and ODDLY enough, Christine Jorgenson had worked at Pathé for a while.

"I really got into the gender biz while working on the Debbie doc. I taped about 75 hours of her story (7 1/2" tape) in which she told of things that happened in Africa when she had the operation, working as a prostitute on 8th Avenue and going to an elderly attorney's office to service him once a week.... Cutting her penis half off and her parents coming home from the movies to find her on the kitchen floor awash in blood.

"My gender-identity doc, *My Name is Debbie*, is (I hear) still being shown around the world with a Canadian film actually showing the male-to-female (m-to-f) operation.

"I was invited to both, Johns Hopkins by John Money who liked the film, AND the King's Cross Training Center in London, and [I] was interviewed there when my movie was screened. After that, I helped

Zelda Suplee with post-op transsexuals when she had an office on 5th Avenue. Some very wealthy TS funded her. Stanley Krippner knows all this. Bob only figures in because it was his idea for me to make the movie and he did advise me on several points. Because of the TS film, a whole bunch of stuff happened in my life, but I won't go into that. Those tapes have gone where the woodbine twineth, of course, along with the many Jean Shepherd tapes that have ALSO disappeared!"

Krippner confirmed this by calling it a pioneering documentary film about an early m-to-f transsexual, which has been shown in classes for decades.

Jeanne's mention of Shepherd intrigued me. Jeanne: "According to author [Shepherd biographer] Eugene Bergmann, Jean Shepherd had given me boxes of his tapes, a thousand and more. Anyway, several boxes. I dated Jean until he met and married Lois Nettleton. I was living on East 83rd Street then. After I married Bob, we took Jean and Lois out to dinner several times. In the 1960s, Jean was in a transitional stage (?) and asked if we could store his tapes as we had room, or maybe he had even given them to us.

"Bob taught/told me how to animate. He knew everything about moviemaking! I did great and sold my films... won an award from the Association Internat du Film Animation... and later segued into documentaries – also Bob's idea.

As regards her involvement in specific aspects of the compilations, such as the music, Jeanne admitted: "I did go with him to some of the music sessions here in New York. I don't know who or which were his favorites."

As far as his choice of Chopin's "Étude in C Major, Opus 10, No. 3," as his theme song for the compilations, Jeanne stated, "I don't know about Chopin. I am interested in gazillions of things but music is not among them. My father did not like to have music on in the house (especially classical), and of course it rubbed off on me. I liked the Big Bands and Elvis... but... well, you get the picture."

Since some of the greats, such as Laurel and Hardy, Buster Keaton, Harold Lloyd, etc., were alive during Youngson's heyday, Jeanne recalled, "As far as I know, Harold Lloyd was the only old timer Bob met. And the only celeb I ever met through Bob was Harold Lloyd – I have a lovely copy of a photo of Harold and me taken at some premiere. What a nice guy he was. He too kept a Christmas tree up all year long, he told me. (I did for a while...)

"Oh, and at one point Hayward Morse stayed in the suite at #1 Fifth when he was doing a stage play on Broadway. He was the son of my friends, Barry and Sydney Morse... Barry played Lt. Gerard in the original *Fugitive*. Hayward is still alive and well in London – but I don't think he had much to do with Bob as their hours would have been different. Just racking my brains for... anyone [that would be able to help you regarding Bob].

"Still, and this is strange, I met lots of film folk when I worked at the MoMA and one day started chatting with an old fella who said he had once been active in the film world. It was Charles Rosher. This would have been about 1961 or so, when I was back at the MoMA on a volunteer basis dispensing info. I told him about Bob's work and invited him down to meet Bob – who seemed singularly unimpressed. To this day, I do not know why. Rosher died in 1974 so this was about 13 years before he passed on.

Bob's greatest idea is probably the compilations for they kept his name alive. Jeanne: "Bob said he got the idea for his compilations when the three of them [his parents and him] were driving cross country to California and he dragged them to movies along the way. He noticed how much people enjoyed the comedies... this would have been in the late 1930s, don't you think? He had not kept in touch with college friends, seldom even mentioned his time at Harvard, in fact.

"Bob could drive and had a license. When we went to Florida to visit my parents in the 1960s, he drove from the airport to the motel we stayed in... but he didn't own any property. I guess he sold his parent's home in Brooklyn. His sister came from California and sent everything of value back."

5

Bob on the Features

"I think the secret of making a compilation is just searching, searching, searching. First, it's hard to uncover; then also, not all silent comedy was great… only a small percentage. To make a poor compilation would be easy."

– Robert Youngson, 1971 Interview,
Film Fan Monthly

IN THE INTERVIEW with *Film Fan Monthly* (*FFM*), Youngson also told of how he came to make the feature compilations of silent film comedies, which revived interest in Laurel and Hardy and silent comedy films.

Youngson: "Back in 1950, when *50 Years Before Your Eyes* came out, I traveled out to the West Coast with my parents by car, and as I went from city to city, my picture would be playing in the local theaters. I went to see it many, many times to test the audience reaction to it, and I had inserted near the beginning of the film a silent comedy sequence with Charlie Chaplin. Invariably this got tremendous response from audiences, which hadn't had the opportunity to see these old silent comedies in years.

"I came back from this tour across the country and tried to convince Warner Brothers to let me make a feature that I called *The Golden Age of Comedy*. For seven years, I tried to make that picture, but no one was interested. Finally, with some financial assistance from a partner, I made that picture. After I made that, I took it around to all the major distributors; I would sit in screening rooms with these people, and they would roar – they would love it. Then they would say, well, we love it, but it isn't the type of thing for audiences – it's too episodic. They just couldn't see any future in that type of film.

"So finally I had to have it distributed by an independent, DCA. It was a slow starter – it wasn't acclaimed overnight – but it gradually built into a very successful film. Fortunately for me 20th Century Fox had taken the foreign rights from DCA, and much to their assessment, it was a tremendous success in other countries. In India, for example, it was the biggest grossing Fox film of that year. So with this success I was able to go to 20th Century Fox with my next film, and ever since then I have had no trouble finding a distributor for my films.

When *FFM* asked if he gathered material over the years for his first compilation, or if he just started in 1957, Youngson said, "Oh no, I had been planning the film in my mind for years, and gathering material. Fortunately I was able to make an arrangement with the Hal Roach studios to use their material, and I also made use of my Mack Sennett footage."

As far as the difficulty in obtaining the footage, Youngson explained: "It worked out very well… it was the same problem I think you would have if you had a sudden inspiration that pebbles on the street were going to be valuable someday, and you went around gathering pebbles off the street. There was absolutely no feeling that these films had any value, at the time; if there had been, there would have been other people [to] make use of the material."

When *FFM* asked if his first compilation, *The Golden Age of Comedy*, was his favorite, Youngson said, "Well, I think it was the breakthrough film; I don't think it's the best. It's very hard to single out one film as a favorite. But it certainly broke new ground – I know at the time Laurel and Hardy were pretty much ignored. I remember it was sort of an act of courage to include so much Laurel and Hardy footage in the feature. I kept testing it and it was always Laurel and Hardy that got the greatest reaction. I was determined that I was going to go by the reactions to a great extent. I found that I had to include so much Laurel and Hardy that in a sense the picture was top-heavy with Laurel and Hardy. At that time, that didn't mean much – they weren't even considered first-rate comedians. Look at James Agee's article 'Comedy's Greatest Era' and you'll find Laurel and Hardy were brushed off. I decided to go ahead and let the film be top-heavy with Laurel and Hardy, and it paid off."

FFM asked, "Looking at your first four silent film compilations *Golden Age of Comedy*, *When Comedy Was King*, *Days of Thrills and Laughter*, and *30 Years of Fun*, what would you say was the biggest problem involved in doing these films?"

Youngson: "Getting the material. I think the secret of making a compilation is just searching, searching, searching. First, it's hard to uncover; then also, not all silent comedy was great... only a small percentage. To make a poor compilation would be easy."

Youngson said that each film takes about a year to make and that year is spent, "mostly finding the material and getting it ready for reproduction as part of the film. Next to that, I would say music scoring takes up a lot of time. Most regular features just have music bridges, and have long stretches without music. These films can't have a second without music."

FFM: "When you went to MGM for *The Big Parade of Comedy*, were you subject to any interference from the studio?"

Youngson: "I'm happy to say no, none whatsoever. But that is the one film of mine that I do not own. I was paid a salary for that one; MGM financed it, and I received 50% of the profits. As part of that contract, however, I was able to make one film on my own which MGM then had rights to distribute, which was *Laurel and Hardy's Laughing 20s*."

As far as problems dealing with excerpts of sound films for *The Big Parade of Comedy*, Youngson revealed, "Very severe, different problems. Sound films are much harder to glue together. I have found that pacing in old films is much different from that of today; consequently, for each of my films I have test screenings. I find where the dead spots are, and I pull a lot together. When dealing with talkies this becomes a lot more difficult, with dialogue and music on the soundtrack – if you cut, there may be a sudden jump in the music, so that presents a serious problem."

FFM asked: "Your latest films have been devoted entirely to Laurel and Hardy; do you think you could have done such a film at the time of *Golden Age of Comedy*?"

Youngson: "I could have done a wonderful Laurel and Hardy film, but it just wouldn't have sold. Outside of kids there seemed to be no adult interest in them at the time; certainly there was no critical interest."

As regards his last compilation film, *4 Clowns*, Charley Chase shares equal billing with Laurel and Hardy and Buster Keaton. *FFM* asked, "Do you think this will mean new recognition for him?"

Youngson: "Well, Charley Chase is in a position now where Laurel and Hardy were ten years ago. And hopefully, I think I even hear rumors of it now – he will come into his own.

Youngson concludes his interview with *FFM* with an appeal for footage, saying: "Actually, I can say that if anybody, anywhere, has any 35mm comedy material, I would like to buy it from them... anything of possible value. I would like to see a lot more of Educational Comedies of the 1920s; some I have seen are bad, but there are some that are quite good. And whereas Laurel and Hardy comedies have managed to survive, we're not nearly as lucky with Charley Chase. I've looked at just about everything that exists on Charley Chase from the silent days, and I think this is about it – unless somebody else has a print of something. There is no problem with rights, because if there are rights I can arrange to buy them from the copyright owner. The only trouble is that so many copyright owners have rights but no films. I hope we can uncover more film and preserve it."

FFM commended Youngson, saying, "Well, you have done more than practically anyone else to achieve this end, and all film buffs are grateful to you for it."

Youngson concluded the interview, saying: "Thank you – you know, everybody has to have a goal in life, and that's my goal, to preserve as much of this great comedy material as possible."

6

The Curtain Lowers, Hail and Farewell

"The 68th St. Playhouse was one of the theatres that played his films. I'd have gone with him to everything he went to. Except when he was out with Al or earlier his Dad, he didn't go anywhere without me. I loved seeing his movies. Still love seeing them. I never heard of anyone who did not like them. Never heard of a controversy about only getting portions of films [in his compilations]. Whenever we went to see them, there was applause at the end."

– Jeanne Keyes Youngson, 2015
Interview with Jim Manago

BACK IN 1998, Jeanne told MacGillivray: "He had diabetes, and wasn't too well.... He was kind of enjoying himself, but I knew he wasn't feeling well."

In 2015, at first Jeanne unequivocally denied that stating, "I don't think there was any diabetes then, or if it was diabetes ever or at all. I will ask my sister, the nurse, the next time she calls. She's in a retirement place in North Carolina, but telephones me when she is feeling up to it.

Jeanne's sister was more certain of Bob's health woes towards the end. Jeanne: "[I talked to my sister now who] says Bob did have diabetes and the old geezer [his family physician] probably did tell him on the phone to double up on his meds when he was feeling poorly.

"However, she said he was probably not well for some time and was in denial, otherwise he'd have gone to an endocrinologist or at the very least a legit physician in Manhattan who had not been the family retainer for 100 years.

"As for being in denial, of course he was, otherwise he would not have eaten as much as he did. [My sister] remembered when she was visiting us back in the 1960s, Bob asked her to go out and get ice cream for the three of us. A pint for her and me and a gallon for him. And he ate the whole gallon."

Everson spoke to MacGillivray about Youngson's health: "It's really a pity that he didn't take better notice of his doctor. He certainly had the money to eat well and properly, and keep within a doctor's diet. He was an extremely large man, and on a number of occasions, he went on a crash diet to lose weight. In fact, just before he got married he went on a crash diet to lose a lot of weight. And then suddenly he'd say the hell with it, and order up about six ice-cream sodas – and polish off the lot in one fell swoop."

Youngson apparently shelved his last project (a ninth compilation) in 1974. Everson told MacGillivray: "He may have lost interest and become a little despondent. That may be one of the reasons why he suddenly said, 'The hell with the doctors, I'm just going to eat what I want.' He was constantly warned by his doctors that this could be fatal, and that's what happened. It's a pity, because there was so much left to him."

Jeanne: "I don't know how you'll handle this, Jim. Here's a bright talented guy, but… flawed? Two things: Money and intake of food. [My sister] remembers the time he got down to a reasonable weight and said he was really a handsome guy.

"And you speak of The End: during the time I knew him, he fluctuated weight-wise A LOT! At one point he was so heavy the back of his legs (skin) began to split and he was in a hospital in the Bronx for a few weeks. He lost a lot of weight after that but put it back on.

"His family had been going to an ancient doctor in Brooklyn forever who [supposedly] told Bob he had diabetes and began medicating him for it. He began staying at #1 Fifth all the time where he had a special bed. The special bed came along in the mid-1960s during one of the times he ballooned up.

"My sister, who as a nurse, told me what to do if he went into a coma, which he did one evening. I called St. Vincent's per instructed and they sent an ambulance PDQ. The attendants told me to gather up all his meds and take them to the hospital, which I did – just a 10-minute walk from #1 Fifth.

"He was in the ICU where he stayed for a couple of weeks and then went into a private room for almost two more weeks.

"He never regained consciousness.

"I spoke with an attorney somewhere along the line and told him that the old doc had told Bob OVER THE PHONE to double up on his meds but the lawyer said anything over the phone was just hearsay, so forget it. I was allowed in the ICU for ten minutes each hour so I went back and forth every day, all day. He died, as you know, on April 15, 1974."

I asked Jeanne, "Did Bob know he was dying?"

Jeanne: "My goodness, no. He had no plans to die. Even though my uncle Charles (an M.D.) gave him seven years (from 1960), he lasted about fourteen. Of course, no one ever told him of Charles' prediction. I suppose Bob thought he would go on forever.

"Did he care about me? I guess [that] after the initial thrill dies down, people often take their mates for granted. I had (and have) a good disposition and with MY love of movies, was convenient to have around. It worked both ways as I had the Dracula Society, a career in animation, lots of friends, volunteering at the MoMA – and always taking classes, etc. I could do what I wanted as long as I was there when he would have been alone. It's a good thing Al was still with him, even though he (Al) was in very poor health. I don't know what would have happened if he'd lost Al. My gal pals were getting divorced right and left so it never occurred to me not to stay with him.

"And I really don't think he ever wondered if I was happy… And yes, he did love film more than anything else."

Jeanne admitted she was indeed stunned when Bob died. Jeanne: "Gosh, no. I didn't expect Bob – from the beginning or ever – to die. I was stunned when it happened. I kept going over to the hospital and talking to him every day, telling him once that the night before on the Oscar-show, there had been a cute clip of him getting one of his Oscars. He grabbed it and yelled 'WOW!' which brought the house down.

"Well, son of a gun! I just had a memory about the funeral. As I told you, my brother and sister were younger than I [was] so they would have been in their 20s when Bob died. Oh, just happened to think that my dad (step-dad) gave me their (my parents) grave site in ye olde hometown, Sussex, N.J., for Bob's interment. Some of my former classmates carried his coffin. Of course, they are all gone now and there he is!

'Since he was to be buried in Clove Cemetery in Sussex, New Jersey, we had to do everything locally. And that's why my classmates, volunteer firemen in the 1970s, carried the casket. So my bro and sis and I went up to choose the coffin and make arrangements for the service and burial."

Youngson's service was held in the Vollmicke Funeral Home, also in Sussex.

Jeanne: "We met at the office by the funeral director and his wife and all the way through the visit, she kept smiling. I couldn't figure it out so as we were leaving, I asked her why the smile. She said we were the youngest people they ever had to make funeral arrangements with them.

"I guess I told you I asked my friend Mark Benecke who was with the New York Coroner's Office what would have happened to Bob if I had not been around when he died... AND my dad hadn't given us their burial plots up in Sussex, New Jersey. Mark said the city would have put him on ice until someone claimed the body. Hmmm...

"Bob wasn't on particularly good terms with his sister who was always after him about The Will. Al wouldn't have had the slightest idea what to do.... Bernie? After the wedding I don't recall Bob even mentioning his name...

"And you and I haven't even discussed the hospital bill for almost a month! After Bob died, the stack of bills from St. Vincent's was over 3 inches tall/high. I don't recall the amount, but that was also paid by the attorney who was paying the other bills I told you about – when the courts took over his bank account.

"Bob didn't have a sense of humor. I used to tease him about writing such funny material... and not being funny in person. Never did a funny thing, never told a joke. He did laugh at the old comedies but I don't remember him chuckling spontaneously at anything. [I] think he was in a sort of time-warp? Born in 1900?"

However, Jeanne told MacGillivray a somewhat different explanation: "He smiled easily and did have a good sense of humor, but I thought he should have been funnier. I remember once telling him, 'You know, your movies are really so humorous, I see them and I laugh. But why aren't you funny in person?' And I think I hurt his feelings, poor guy."

Jeanne confessed to me, "I guess it sounds like Bob wasn't very good husband material. However, I did have animation and later the documentaries, and got recognition for them. I was also able to travel and there were other perks along the way. My personal funds ran out at about the time he died which meant I had to rely on my parents to tide me oven when the courts prevailed. It was really nice of my dad to give me the cemetery plot(s) for him. Hmmm...

As far as Bob's belongings, Jeanne remembered: "Al did take Bob's three pinball machines but as far as I know, not much else. I never saw Bob play pinball. Maybe they meant something to him, like [*Citizen Kane's*] Rosebud, maybe.

"I don't know where scripts or other printed materials would be or might have gone. By that time, Alex Gildzen [Curator at Kent State University Library] picked up the newsreels. Boy, they will have gone back to the early days! What remained of Bob's stuff (including his large collection of films) had been moved down to my new apartment on the third floor at # 1 Fifth. There must have been papers and other printed materials but Al had seen to them. I'm sure he didn't take them. There were HUNDREDS of newsreels that took up several shelves in the steel cabinet which were sent to Kent State University."

As far as survivors, Jeanne said Bob had a "nephew & niece. I've asked Catherine, Carole Anne's daughter (who contacted me last year) to ask her mom if she remembers anything about 'Uncle Bobby?' I'll let you know if and when she replies. I have no idea where the boy is."

Later Jeanne mused as Bob's only surviving relatives offered no help. Jeanne: "Confidential… plot thickens.

"The money issue is complicated. His dad was a used car salesman so there was no money from the Youngson family, or so you'd think. Harvard? Well, for sure tuition was less than now. If (his mom) Carrie's folks could afford to take her to Europe, maybe they helped him out?

"He bought me the animation stand, the 16mm camera and film, but otherwise gave me almost no spending money. But that was OK as I had my wardrobe from working at MCA and we did almost everything together. I had my own money for traveling when he went to California. And did this come in handy when the courts took over after he died without the joint bank account. I had to go further into my savings for food and personal expenses.

"The court-appointed attorney paid the rent on two apartments & utilities and caught up with Bob's bills. If I hadn't had money and family to help me out, I'd have been in real trouble.

"Bob would not open a joint bank account. His sister nagged him about leaving money to her two kids. And when the will was read, he had split his 'estate' three ways. I was told that since we did not have a joint account, the courts would appoint an attorney to pay all the bills until things had been straightened out. That meant a lawyer had access to Bob's bank account and he paid rent on the apartment at #1 Fifth, the penthouse, all utilities as well as other outstanding bills. And of course, he got a – percentage? Not a pretty picture.

"Ah, yes. That will. It was split three ways. After the courts took that sizable chunk to pay bills, I, of course, got a reasonable amount of money. My friends, the aforementioned Barry Morse's, offered me their flat in London while they went to Australia to be in "Hadrian the 7th" and I spent the next several years sort of commuting. [I] gave up animation when the Dracula society got so big… "

Jeanne told MacGillivray: "I know that Robert was very attached to his full-length films, because before he died he did see his name in the books as a pioneer of a certain kind. Some of them are a little [backhanded] about it, you know, saying that his stuff wasn't very professional and really wasn't very good. But we know different, don't we?"

Jeanne established a scholarship in memory of Bob. Jeanne: "I endowed a film scholarship at the New School for Social Research in memory of Robert Youngson." However, I pointed out to her that the middle initial is wrong; it should be "Robert G. Youngson" not as it is listed, "Robert M. Youngson." Jeanne: "I guess after all this time Bob's initial can't be changed. Yes, it's 'G.' The guy I met regarding the scholarship was so nice. He said something like, 'I think it is wonderful that you as a young widow are donating all this money so your husband will be remembered.' I wasn't 50 yet. He also said something about the New School expanding radically which was a surprise as it was such a cute little college.

Bob's obituary ("Robert Youngson, Producer, 56, Who Won 2 Oscars in 50's, Dies") noted, "The Freedom Foundation awarded him its George Washington medal for making 'an outstanding contribution to our way of life.' "

Jeanne: "He was pleased to have received the Freedom Foundation Award, I know. He seldom mentioned anything that happened before we met although he did tell me he was impressed to meet Eisenhower's brother when he got that one award.

"He didn't have much interest in politics, religion, social beliefs. No military service. Somewhere along the line, didn't Bob write stuff for the war effort?

Undoubtedly, Jeanne offered her most telling remark about her husband when she said to me in passing, "Bob seemed to live in the moment, come to think of it."

Part Two

Robert Youngson's Films

7

Before His Independence

"The point is that this is not merely a case of slapping film together or of ridiculing old-fashioned techniques but an honest effort to present outstanding old movies, which may have been forgotten over the years, in the best possible way."

– Robert Youngson on his 1957 re-release
of 1929's *Noah's Ark*

BEFORE HE BECAME an independent producer/writer, Youngson made dozens of short subjects, six of them were nominated for awards by the Academy of Motion Picture Arts and Sciences.

MacGillivray summed them up: "The Youngson shorts looked back at 'the era of wonderful nonsense,' focusing on bygone celebrities, headline news events, sports heroes, politicians, daredevils, crackpot inventors, and everyday people."

Everson told MacGillivray: "That trilogy on World War I – *This Was Yesterday*, *It Happened to You*, and *Those Exciting Days* – is a wonderful group of films, and a wonderful piece of historical reconstruction, rescuing a lot of the very, very best Pathé newsreel footage at a time when nobody else was paying attention to it.

"Not just the historical subjects, but the political reels like *I Never Forget A Face*. Even when he was dealing with sports or motor racing, it was always put into a kind of context. He really didn't give a damn about sports, but he always tried to give it a sick sense of humor. His films on auto racing and skiing are full of the most horrendous spills and thrills!

"He was looking at a lot of negatives at Warner Brothers, and he would often run off silent features that he thought might make interesting one-reel condensations. I think he arrived in that field [of silent-film revivals] just a little bit too early, when it was not yet fully accepted. I know his bosses at Warners didn't like it too much when he did one-reel cut-downs from silent films. They felt 'one out of every ten is all we can allow you to do.' He had a free hand on what he did, but if he tried to do more of the one-reel cutdowns of silents, they would have probably stopped him."

The first mention of Youngson in the *Los Angeles Times* was on February 12, 1951 with an announcement for his Warner Brothers one-reeler (1000 feet or less) production called *Blaze Dusters*.

The following year, Youngson's one-reeler, *The World of Kids* was among the nominations for an Academy Award (*Los Angeles Times*, February 12, 1952), and he won the award in the ceremony on March 20, 1952. Why the 34-year old Youngson did not attend the ceremonies is unknown. Lucille Ball announced the nominations and the winner. Up stepped Cedric Francis (1915-2003), associated with Warner Brothers Short Subject Department, to accept the award. Francis accepted the Oscar saying, "On behalf of Mr. Youngson, a very, very warm thank you!"

Everson told MacGillivray: "I remember I was with him on his 35th birthday [1950], and he suddenly said, 'My God, do you realize in fifteen years I'll be 50? For him, that was the end of the world!"

Youngson's one-reeler, *This Mechanical Age*, described as, "a history of aviation that provided both humor and pathos" (*Los Angeles Times*, February 13, 1955). And he won the award on March 30, 1955.

One of Youngson's two-reelers got press coverage on April 30, 1955. *New York Times*: "Just as colorful, and in its way quite important, is a seventeen-minute Warner short subject that rounds out the Plaza's program. Titled *When the Talkies Were Young*, this Robert Youngson production shows vintage clips from *Sinners Holiday* (1930) with James Cagney and Joan Blondell; *20,000 Years in Sing Sing* (1933), with Spencer Tracy and Bette Davis; *Night Nurse* (1931) with Barbara Stanwyck and Clark Gable; *Svengali* (1931) with John Barrymore and *Five-Star Final* (1931) with Edward G. Robinson. To all movie historians, amateur or otherwise: Don't walk, run!"

The following year Youngson's one-reeler, *Gadgets Galore* received a nomination for an Academy Award (*Los Angeles Times*, February 19, 1956).

On September 11, 1956, Studio Films, Inc. announced that they acquired the Warner Bros. subsidiary that produced Pathé newsreels and shorts. With Benjamin Frye as President of Pathé Pictures, and Youngson, as production chief of Warners free-of-charge educational film series for children *News Magazine of the Screen*, now became one of the vice presidents. Youngson is credited on 81 monthly issues of *News Magazine of the Screen*. According to the *New York Times*, the series reached some 20 million U.S. children a year in the early 1950s. In addition, he edited the Classroom Guide to the series.

New York Times: "Although the Warner Pathé newsreel was discontinued on Aug. 23, Pathé Pictures which reportedly paid about $500,000 for the newsreel library, cameras and installations of Warner News will acquire more than 22,000,000 feet of newsreel footage dating back to 1898."

"While Pathé Pictures will not produce newsreels for theatres, the present plan, according to Mr. Frye, is to use the vast Pathé library for the production of television documentaries and news subjects, and theatrical short subjects, as well as for the successful two-reel documentaries of the *News Magazine of the Screen*. Many of these subjects have been distributed to schools throughout the country."

Under Youngson's control, Warners produced 38 theatrical short subjects.

The next year, *I Never Forget a Face*, a one-reeler produced by Youngson for Warner Brothers, is announced on February 8, 1957 in *Los Angeles Times*.

On March 10, 1957, *New York Times*' A. H. Weiler reported, "There's life in the old ones. Last week it was learned that Robert Youngson, the Hal Roach Studios and Associated Artists have very quietly turned out over the last five months 'a modern sound adaptation' of Warner Brothers' 1929 *Noah's Ark*. The two-hour feature had Darryl Zanuck as the writer, and Michael Curtiz as the director. It included such stars as Dolores Costello, George O'Brien and Noah Beery. This combination of Biblical spectacle and modern story, largely a silent film, also had a few talking sequences.

"Mr. Youngson, who has won Academy Awards for short subjects, said that the film had been edited to seventy-minute length and had no dialogue now. 'I wrote a narration, which is spoken off-screen by Dwight Weist and which explains the changes in acting styles over the years. An entirely new sound track, music score and sound effects have been worked in also. 'The point is,' he added, 'that this is not merely a case of slapping film together or of ridiculing old-fashioned techniques but an honest effort to present outstanding old movies, which may have been forgotten over the years, in the best possible way.'"

In a *Los Angeles Times* article, "Old *Noah's Ark* Still Wettest Picture of All," September 27, 1957, Philip K. Scheuer, criticized the re-release of the two million dollar spectacle silent film. Scheuer: "*Noah's Ark* was pretty much of a wet blanket 29 years ago, and it hasn't dried out with age. The same picture is back... with continuous narration replacing the stilted dialogue of the original, which was part talkie. Robert Youngson is responsible for the 'new' production, whose value is quite simply, that of a curio piece.

"...The special effects by Fred Jackman range from awesome to plain awful. They spent thousands to soak the audience in the Biblical Deluge and then stinted on a train wreck, in the 'modern' story, that I could improve upon in my back yard with my daughter's toys.... But just as the gloss has faded from the original, so whatever life they may have suggested has left the pantomiming, posturing players. Shadow figures, indeed – bloodless, removed and a little Pathétic."

An ad on September 28, 1957, *Los Angeles Times*, described the re-release of the 1928 silent film *Noah's Ark* as, "THE GREATEST SPECTACLE OF ALL TIME" AND *Noah's Ark* and THE FLOOD THAT DESTROYED THE WORLD!" Youngson received credit for "Special Adaptation."

Everson told MacGillivray: "He loved his own words on screen, and would *never* cut them. Even when both friends *and* preview cards complained about unnecessary narration, he took no notice – and it got worse. The nadir was his version of *Noah's Ark*, where he even gave God new dialogue and rewrote the Bible. But at least you could kid Bob about all that and make your feelings plain. He didn't mind the criticism. He always had an answer, and was always sure he was right. He just smiled and did it his own way."

The original production of *Noah's Ark* came out at the time when the studios started to make sound pictures. The 135-minute Warner Brothers spectacle costing over a million dollars to make was planned as a silent film for release in 1927, but it got added sound as a part-talkie version when it got released in 1928 utilizing the Vitaphone sound on disc system. After its premiere, it was edited down to 108 minutes. Although the sound version still had intertitles, it had the advantage of offering some scenes with dialogue, as well as sound effects and a synchronized full orchestral music score.

The film moves between the Biblical story of Noah and the Great Flood to a parallel modern story of a train derailment that takes place on the eve and during World War I. Both stories end optimistically, as humanity receives a new hope after the Biblical Flood and a hope that the signing of the Armistice ending World War I might end war for good.

Dolores Costello, George O'Brien, Noah Beery and Myrna Loy are among the stars playing dual roles in both stories under the direction of Curtiz. The film turned a profit, grossing nearly twice its cost, but it also caused a number of injuries with at least three extras drowned. Even lead female Costello contracted pneumonia. This led to safety regulations not too long after its release.

Youngson saw the film's value in the many scenes with superb special effects, and so he focused on those scenes in his 75-minute version. In 1957, the film's re-release through Dominant Pictures Corporation appeared as a more effectively tightened silent film with added narration.

8

The Comedy Compilations

"People don't realize what a vast amount of comedies were turned out then. Some were good, others bad; working with it is like a treasure hunt. At no time in the history of movies did so many young comedians come up at the same time, from vaudeville, carnivals, burlesque and circus. Their product was made by youth and many died young. When they left no one came along to replace them."

– Robert Youngson quoted by
Hedda Hopper, May 24, 1960

WHAT IS MOST EVIDENT to anyone watching Youngson's compilations of silent film comedies is the clear sense that the tone of those films constantly returns to a nostalgic yearning for a bygone era. There's an unforgettable pathos, an inescapable sadness, in each film, particularly at the close as Youngson's narrator expresses how the comics and the days as depicted in the film are now long gone.

Considerably effective in capturing that tone is the superb use of Chopin's Étude at the start and finish of each compilation, and sometimes during some of the film clips. Though untitled by Chopin when he wrote it for piano in 1832 as an exercise for piano students, song lyrics have been offered several times in the 20th century. Often it has been entitled "Tristesse," which could be described as sadness.

Youngson explained to *FFM* how he came to select his main musical theme: "Well, I had heard that Chopin Étude when I was a kid, and when

I was a kid I was always having fantasies of making motion pictures, and in my fantasies I had decided upon this as the theme. It took all those years, when I finally made *The Golden Age of Comedy*, to give me the opportunity to use that Chopin Étude. I think it expresses a nostalgic mood, and works very well."

Although it can be argued otherwise, Youngson's scripted narration has been criticized for there was too much of it as well as being overdone. Everson seemed to be the chief critic in this regard. In the program notes for a March 21, 1975 "Tribute to Robert G. Youngson." Everson noted, "If there was one shortcoming in Bob's work, it was that his stunning ability as an editor was partially offset by a tendency to over-write. Like many autonomous writer-producers (Mankiewicz and Preston Sturges would be other parallel examples) Bob, who was a good writer, hated to sacrifice a word of what he had written. He could turn a very neat phrase, and one that seemed particularly apt, he would use again – and again – in subsequent films.

'He was a believer in honest sentiment, and sometimes it got a little out of hand. He also liked to be informative; and in addition, hated for audiences that might not be familiar with the grammar of silent film to miss subtle nuances, so he tended to tell them a little too much.

"The narrations were never snide or smart-alecky; there was just too much of it, especially in his features. If I seem to belabor this point, it is because it will become rather apparent this evening. In just one Youngson short, where the breathless pace of narration and picture mesh, it might not be too apparent. And of course, it was never intended that so many shorts ever be shown together commercially, so I stress this shortcoming as much in fairness to Bob Youngson as in criticism of him."

The problem with this criticism is that it ignores Youngson's experience and filmmaking method that came from that experience. As a newsreel writer and producer, Youngson could not present just raw footage of news events. That would not have any interest to audiences, nor is it the way anyone made newsreels. The process of making a newsreel involves the selection of the real life event footage. Then it is edited in such a way to get right to the intended slant or viewpoint. In addition, the narration that anyone writes for a newsreel is crucial, as it must drive a certain point home effectively in as few words as possible.

Everson the film scholar did not fully appreciate Youngson's experience and training in writing newsreels. Youngson had learned how to grab an audience with words, whether they are explanatory, and/or humorous. The briefness of newsreels meant the footage and narration had to be strong as these productions were meant to be tight. There is no gratuitous footage or wasted words. There is no escaping the fact that Youngson brought that tremendous experience and skill in making newsreels from Pathé with him, and most certainly, he applied it to his own compilations of silent comedy footage when he became an independent producer in 1958.

If Youngson had just clipped scenes together without overlapping them with clever talk, then it would have been just as useless in making a newsreel made up of edited raw footage of events without any substantial narration. It would be ludicrous to think the audience would get something meaningful from the resultant film. Such a production composed of some edited clips of fictional movies without substantial narration is just as unentertaining and a waste of the audiences' attention as making a newsreel made up of raw footage of real events without giving a real punch via a well-written narration.

Both newsreels and the fictional film compilations gain much from the selective editing and added narration. When one makes either film form, it would be wise to do it intelligently and correctly, the editor works at making a production that overcomes the possible blandness of the film clips. Indeed, carefully chosen words delivered by a good narrator impart to the finished product a distinct point of view, even if it is added just as a signpost to steer audiences to what this all means. Besides that, it heightens the enjoyment, especially if the words are humorous and light. Youngson never stopped using such techniques developed in making superb newsreels.

Simply put, Everson did not understand Youngson's need to do the compilations the way he did them. No one can ever deny or underestimate the value of Everson's life-long study and scholarship, and his enormous contribution to film history. However, what he seemed to want from Youngson is for him to say little as far as narration. Literally, he should just provide the footage of the silent comedians and step aside. This obfuscates Youngson's desire and need to properly inform and condition his audiences about what he learned in going through thousands of comedy shorts of the 1920s.

Youngson just could not ignore telling everything he could about the silent film comedians and their complete mastery of visual humor. He may have been unsure if all of his audience would have much knowledge of the meaning of it all or grasp the subtleties at work. So he felt compelled to explain some things by adding comments that may seem to be superfluous.

However, Everson seemed to have missed something here; perhaps that is why Youngson ignored his criticism. It does seem; however that by the time of his last compilations he did seem less obvious in describing the actions being shown in the clips. In addition, there does seem to be some diminution of witty narration after his third compilation.

Undoubtedly, whether one likes it or not, Youngson's compilations (particularly the first three in my opinion) are so powerful in drawing viewers literally into his worldview. He achieved that simply by scripting some witty lines and having good narrators deliver them melded over the comedy footage he so painstakingly selected.

In retrospect, what makes Youngson's productions worth viewing then and now is the added wit that he brought to them by his superb writing (even granted you want to call it "overwriting" at times). That makes them productions worthy of sharing with each new generation of film audiences.

Critics have said that the scenes selected by Youngson were funny already, and they did not need the added silly sound effects besides Youngson's verbal comedy. Understandably, these silent film purists cannot help but be troubled by Youngson's predilection for adding sound effects and his own verbal comedy to his compilations.

Oftentimes Youngson bears criticism here; however, it really is a misunderstanding of the film compilation form. Indeed, the film excerpts do not need anything to be funnier. But the truth is that often the Youngson method of creating his compilations is at odds with what the purist really hopes for (which is just the films uncut and unadulterated). Again, what makes the compilations so memorable, even more enjoyable, and worth re-seeing, is that they are not just comedy scenes spliced together that unfolds. Youngson created a skeleton of sound effects and verbal comedy that the comedy excerpts hang onto and fit together to make a whole that is much greater than the total of all the parts.

Others have denigrated Youngson for carelessly damaging the original films. This is also an unfair criticism. MacGillivray: "Some film buffs have questioned Robert Youngson's archival methods, claiming that he copied only those scenes he intended to use, allowing the rest of the negative to degenerate. This may have been true when Youngson was extracting one brief clip out of a six-reel feature, but not when he worked with a Hal Roach two-reeler."

Everson told MacGillivray: "In most cases he'd preserve the whole thing, because he was never sure when he might want to come back to it later and handle it differently. He would sometimes screen negative, just to see what he had, and then make workprints of that material.

"He'd invested in one of the labs, and he had a lot of regular income coming in from labs. He was an extremely good businessman.

"He was constantly busy on something. He was always acquiring film. I remember there was one Fatty Arbuckle film which was never released called *Leap Year*, which I had access to, and which he fell in love with when he saw it. He wanted very much to use it, and spent a lot of money making a new negative and prints from it. I don't think he ever used a foot of it in any of the films. I know he was always very disappointed at audience reaction to what he thought was very funny Arbuckle footage. So an awful lot of time went into screening and preparing between releases."

Some of his early work in newsreels did not get the attention in retrospectives back in the 1950s with the exception of those film societies such as the Huff Society that showed them. *A Bit of the Best*, is a title, which got press mention as part of the Cinema 16 program held in the auditorium of the Museum of Modern Art in New York City in *New York Times* on December 7, 1956.

Also, Stuart Legg's color documentary, *The Rival World*; a French documentary, *The End of the Night*; the Dutch film *Maskerage*; an Italian film, *From Movement to Music*; a Swedish experimental film, *Hallucinations* were among the titles sharing the bill that night with Youngson's short.

The story is often told that Youngson's first silent comedy film compilation came about due to his early feature-length documentary for Warners in 1950, *Fifty Years Before Your Eyes* (narrated by Arthur Godfrey, Dwight Weiss and others) The film covered historical events from 1900 to 1950, including natural and man-made disasters, and political matters involving William McKinley, Theodore Roosevelt, etc. It did not stand out as a great accomplishment for Youngson, except in that he remembered the excellent response audiences gave to a Chaplin slapstick sequence (from *His New Job*) in that film.

This inspired him to develop an entire film of slapstick culled from the thousands of shorts that existed from the silent days. Youngson told Hopper in an article published May 24, 1960: "I'd sit in the theater and the audience would go mad when we hit the slapstick part."

Youngson would talk to Hopper about some of the great silent comedians, saying, "Oliver Hardy was wonderful." To that Hopper explained, "These men worked humbly and many unnoticed for years. Youngson will tell you of Babe Hardy's patient grind from 1915 to 1926 playing villains for Hal Roach before he was 'discovered.' Stan Laurel was starred in the 20s but the miracle happened, only when the big fat man and the skinny one were teamed and an incredible comic rapport and fury ensued."

Youngson: "They had a background of failure and great humility. Success came when a *New York Times* editorial described them as Stan playing against fat Oliver like a bow against a fiddle, producing wondrous music. Hardy never read it; it was written after his death. It came late for Stan, too; he'd been ill for a long time, still is."

Youngson said that Charlie Chaplin: "became the vogue, the yardstick by which all others were measured. His followers were so prejudiced other comedians suffered." He told Hopper: "Fatty Arbuckle, who came from the carnivals, was a marvelous comic who directed his own pictures and was a true artist. In *Fatty and Mabel Adrift* there is a tender moment where he kisses sleeping Mabel Normand on the brow. You don't see him, just the projection of his silhouette. His techniques were sure, his timing and sense of contrast infallible.

"…Buster Keaton came from the circus. Joe Keaton would throw the kid around the way you toss a football; would fling him into the audience for laughs and they'd throw him back. The advent of sound threw Buster for a time but TV reactivated his art and today he's going strong."

"…The comedians were always shabby little men, the clowns of failure who had tremendous identification with the audience. In those days villains wore the top hats and tails."

9

The Breakthrough

"Well, I think it was the breakthrough film; I don't think it's the best. It's very hard to single out one film as a favorite. But it certainly broke new ground – I know at the time Laurel and Hardy were pretty much ignored. I remember it was sort of an act of courage to include so much Laurel and Hardy footage in the feature."

– Robert Youngson on *The Golden Age of Comedy*,
Film Fan Monthly, 1971

THE TIME ARRIVED for Youngson as an independent producer to do an entire feature-length compilation film of slapstick shorts, as he could never convince Warner Brothers to such a concept. It was not a new idea for the studio as they had done two-reel compilations of such films before. However, the idea of a full feature-length film was untenable to them.

As far as Youngson's first such feature compilation released at the end of 1957 (but usually credited as 1958), *The Golden Age of Comedy*, Everson told MacGillivray that it was "tremendously important because it brought back all the Sennett and Roach material, which nobody had seen. It literally revitalized Laurel & Hardy, and led to a tremendous new interest in silent films, silent comedy in particular."

Everson explained in a book on the team, "Laurel & Hardy's features and shorts have never stopped playing, although often in abominably mutilated and confusingly retitled versions, both in theatres and on TV, but it is to *The Golden Age of Comedy* that most of the credit must go for a renaissance of real interest in the work of Laurel & Hardy, both from the public and from the critics.

"A compilation of great sight gag material from the 20s, primarily from the Roach and Sennett stables, it devoted approximately half of its running time to generous samplings of outstanding silent Laurel & Hardy comedies. Footage that was fresh because it had lain unseen for so long astonished laughter-convulsed audiences with the scope and variety of their comedy – and surprised them with the flawless pictorial quality achieved by printing from the original negatives."

Youngson offers separate title cards for each part of the film presenting the sections as if it was a theater presentation of acts: In *Act One: The Laugh Factory*, there is the Mack Sennett comedies. In *Act Two: Nobody Liked Them But The Public*, the first of three helpings of early Laurel and Hardy comedies; in *Act Three: The Cowboy Who Became a Legend*, humorist Will Rogers; in *Act Four: Two Unforgotten Girls*, a tribute to two actresses whose careers were tragically cut short; Carole Lombard and Jean Harlow; and in *Act Five: The Great Actor*, Ben Turpin's Mack Sennett shorts.

In *Act Six: A Comedy Classic*, we have a second helping of Laurel and Hardy's films. In *Act Seven: So Funny, So Sad*, Harry Langdon. In *Act Eight: Animal Comedy*, amazing animal talents are presented; including, Cameo the Wonder Dog, Puzzums the Cat, and the studio lion with the human stars including Billy Bevan, Charley Chase, Andy Clyde, Harry Gribbon and Kewpie Morgan. In *The Finale: Two Men On a Street*, we close with Laurel and Hardy.

Before the opening credits, the narrator intones over various film clips of Bevan, Langdon, and Laurel & Hardy: "Turn back with us now. Turn back to a time when the movies were much younger, and like all youthful things full of fun and high spirits. Down that long, dusty road the clowns are coming. The great voiceless, irreplaceable clowns who rocked the world with laughter. Most of them are gone. But they have left their shadows behind. So come back with us now. Come back to that time of wonderful nonsense called the 'Roaring 20s.' Come back to the Golden Age of Comedy."

The nostalgic and underlying sad tone throughout *The Golden Age of Comedy* is obvious as the narration reminds us of those performers who tragically are no longer alive, including Lombard and Langdon. On Lombard: "But all things must go. And soon it will be gone as the age of flappers and flaming youth is gone. And a girl named Jane Peters, who became Carole Lombard, and who loved life so well and died so tragically."

On Langdon: "...one of the funniest but saddest screen comedians... This short film was made by Harry Langdon in 1924 when he was at the threshold of international success. Within five years, his comedy instincts seemed to fail. And he rode a rough toboggan to obscurity, heartbreak, and an early death. A close associate summed it up: 'The little fellow was the most tragic figure I ever came across in show business.'"

Although it may be of some interest to detail every scene in Youngson's groundbreaking production, it probably would be better (especially less tedious for the reader) to specify selected moments in the compilation. Among the best sequences in the production that deserve some detailing is the animal comedy scenes.

For instance in one excerpt Chase unknots a caged lion's tail (*The Sting of Stings*). Then he takes a thorn out of the bottom of the lion's paw. We are amused when the lion thankfully puts his paw through the iron caging and pats Chase on his head.

There is Clyde strangely playing a game of checkers with an unnamed cat (*His Unlucky Night*). Actually, it is a famous cat named Puzzums (see Appendix). Narrator: "When Andy Clyde ran out of human companions for checkers, he called on the family cat. Andy also showed why cats aren't used more often for this purpose." Narrator feigning Clyde's voice: "They're too darn good!" Then when he loses to Puzzums, the narrator expresses Clyde's annoyance: "That blain cat, I'll cut down on her milk!"

In addition, Youngson brings us Cameo, a wonderful dog that anyone would want to own (see Appendix) who helps his master catch card players cheating (*Nip and Tuck*). He sits on the table and spies the cards of other players (Morgan and Gribbon), and gives the heads up to his Master (Bevan) to let him know whether to place a bet on the move or not. Narrator: "Gribbon's being outwitted by an adversary with short hair, thick spots and a sawed-off tail." Even though Cameo is chased off the table when it seems he is helping Bevan, the narrator explains: "Under the table Cameo works his wicked wiles." The humor continues in this vein.

Then at the conclusion of a chase sequence that follows, the narrator observes, "In the 20s when this film was made a dog called Rin Tin Tin was one of the most successful stars in films. Little Cameo was never to reach the heights of movie fame, but he could do everything that Rinnie could do and maybe more. Why Rin Tin Tin never snatched a skirt in his life!"

Of course, Cameo is not chasing skirts but pulled off a woman's skirt as a ploy to get the attention of cops to help apprehend the dishonest Morgan and Gribbon, as well as rescue his Master Bevan.

After the chase for the money, the three card players make amends and decide to split it. After Cameo rescues the money from a turtle descending in a pond, the Wonder Dog surprises all (including the viewer) when he runs over to drop the money in a Salvation Army kettle. Narrator: "Three slickers turned suckers stare in horror as little Cameo writes the perfect end to this story by proving that maybe the world should go to the dogs."

Youngson's references in *The Golden Age of Comedy* are to the type of comedies that are "long gone" and we are told we are seeing things in these shorts that happened "so long ago."

From the beginning of the film, we learn the importance of this form of comedy. The narrator tells us that Sennett was the father of American screen comedy. It is a comedy that the studio produced which was "delightfully improbable. Their trade was completely visual, a form of wit that has all but disappeared from the land. But one which experts now agree is perhaps the most imaginative and enduring comedy of all time."

Of special interest here is that Youngson brings us the origins of a famous gag made so familiar to us by Lou Costello. We see a scene with Bevan prepared to enjoy a bowl of oyster stew, but instead he finds himself battling a wild oyster (*Wandering Willies*).

Besides showing us funny sequences of the better known Langdon and Laurel & Hardy in shorts that were unseen since their first theatrical release, Youngson brings us many other hilarious scenes selected from the comedies of the little remembered comics; including Madeline Hurlock, Charlie Murray, Bevan, Morgan, Rogers, and Turpin.

An array of silent film comic players is in Youngson's first parade of comedy film excerpts. Specifically, we see Bevan in his shorts *Super-Hooper-Dyne Lizzies* (1925), *Circus Today* (1926), and *Nip and Tuck* (1923). Langdon is seen in *Remember When?* (1925), and *Luck o' the Foolish* (1924). Laurel & Hardy's shorts shown include *Angora Love* (1929), *Habeas Corpus* (1928), *The Second Hundred Years* (1927), *Double Whoopee* (1929), *We Faw Down* (1928), *You're Darn Tootin'* (1927), *Two Tars* (1928), and *The Battle of the Century* (1927).

In addition, Rogers is seen in his *Going to Congress* (1924), *Uncensored Movies* (1923), and *Big Moments from Little Pictures* (1924). There is Chase in *The Sting of Stings* (1927); Clyde in *His Unlucky Night* (1928); Lombard in *Run, Girl, Run* (1928); and Turpin in *The Jolly Jilter* (1927), *A Harem Knight* (1926), *Yukon Jake* (1924), *Ten Dollars or Ten Days* (1924), *The Prodigal Bridegroom* (1926), and *The Daredevil* (1923). Also seen are Alice Day, Harlow, Thelma Hill, Daphne Pollard, and Jack Richardson.

As far as Youngson utilizing one of Laurel & Hardy's rarest shorts, *The Battle of the Century,* Everson told MacGillivray (ruefully): "It was a *terribly* disappointing short. The first part was actually quite dull. [Youngson] had actually almost written it off when the pie fight came on. And even the pie-fight wasn't terribly well organized. In his final version, he recut it and gave it much more punch."

MacGillivray noted, "It was one of the few times Youngson would rearrange the sequence of shots in a film. The original film was showing signs of decay, and Youngson decided to streamline the sequence, removing damaged or redundant footage and tightening the action to three riotous minutes. George Steiner's inspired musical setting, an orchestration of 'Pop Goes The Weasel,' was a stroke of genius."

Youngson's entry of his first compilation into theaters did not come with a prestigious distributor. *The Golden Age of Comedy* entered via Distributors Corporation of America (DCA), a subsidiary of the British-based The Walter Reade Organization. DCA is best known for distributing low budget films made for drive-ins (including such stinkers as *Plan 9 From Outer Space*).

MacGillivray: "The Company, unsure of how to sell Robert Youngson's 'unusual' picture, planted a publicity item about comedian Andy Clyde in the present tense! Frame enlargements from the film were passed off as current human-interest photos, showing suburbanite 'Mr. Andy Clyde' playing checkers with a cat."

On December 22, 1957, Youngson appeared on *The Steve Allen Show* showing clips of Laurel & Hardy, Lombard, and Rogers. He also received a week of attention on Jack Paar's nightly program.

The February 3, 1958 issue of *Life* offered a photo spread on Youngson's breakthrough, entitled "Sight Gag Revival." It offered two pages of stills from silent films. Youngson framed the article, which was among his belongings donated by Jeanne to Kent State University.

The text (with references to photo locations) stated, "The camera as a vehicle for humor reached a peak almost 30 years ago when, in the silent film comedies, the art of the sight gag flourished. The jokes had to be seen, not heard, and to meet this new challenge the movie-makers produced what many people consider the funniest pictures ever filmed. Now, some of the finest sight gags of the old days have been brought together in a film, *The Golden Age of Comedy,* which Producer Robert Youngson made after looking at some 2,000 comedies.

"Often composed on the spot by the director, comedian, and even the crew as it was put on film, the sight gag violated all laws of nature (left).

Everything that lived or could be moved was loaded with perversity, ready to pop out at the comedian. Even the lowly oyster attacked him from the midst of its own oyster stew (far right) and to a flying pie nothing was sacred (below). But despite everything, the silent comedian displayed an aplomb that could brush off any indignity and jaunty courage enough to pull him through any adversity – any, that is, but the coming of sound that killed the sight gag."

The article pictured the following:

> "A Physical Impossibility is shown in absurd sight gag as a horde of cops appear to be swallowed up behind pile of narrow barrels, then emerge in a truck far too big to have been hidden there."

> "Irritated Oyster eats Billy Bevan's crackers, then squirts back when Billy tries to eat him."

> "Fashionable lady receives direct hit with mushy custard pie in Laurel and Hardy's *Battle of the Century*, in which more than 1,000 custard pies were demolished, an all-time record."

> "A man expectantly waiting for his portrait to be taken gets smashed in the face with a pie."

> "Reduced to same pair of pants, Laurel and Hardy do a walk-off in step."

Of course, all of the unexpected positive response to the film entailed that DCA would re-do their ad campaign for the film, this time including many raves from critics.

Jeanne told MacGillivray: "He always had a fond feeling for the first one. Just looking at his face, when the movie was on and people would laugh, was well worth the price of admission."

One of the ads for Youngson's first compilation of silent comedies appeared in *New York Times*, December 29, 1957. It stated, "Any age is the golden age for... *The Golden Age of Comedy*." It added, "THESE ARE THE LAUGHS THAT MADE THE ROARING 20's ROAR!"

The film had screenings daily at two theaters in New York. There were seven showings a day beginning at 12:20 p.m. (last one starting at 10:25 p.m.)

at the Guild 50th in Rockefeller Center (33 West 50th Street) and continuous showings beginning at 11:45 a.m. at the Embassy 46th on Broadway (B'way & 46th Street). The ad noted, "Children under 12 - 50 cents at all times."

The ad in *New York Times*, January 9, 1958, stated, "Everybody... but EVERYBODY likes *The Golden Age of Comedy*." It offered excerpts from 7 publications, as follows:

> "Gorgeous absurdities!... Satirical slapstick!... Heedless impishness!" – *N.Y. Herald Tribune*

> "JUMPS AND EXPLODES AND RACES!... Laurel and Hardy, Ben Turpin, Harry Langdon have their finest moments!" – *New York Post*

> "The producer deserves an automatic debt of gratitude!" – *New York Times*

> "An enriching feature!" *N.Y. Jour.-Amer.*

> "Prodigious falls! Wild chases! A scoop of nostalgia!" – *N.Y. World-Tele.*

> "A LAUGH TREAT!... The greatest list of star comedians ever, in the best comedy bits of their long careers!" *N.Y. Daily News*

> "HILARIOUS!... ROBUST HOWLS" – *N.Y. Daily Mirror*

The New York Times' critic Bosley Crowther seemed mystified by *The Golden Age of Comedy*, and he somehow could not get what Youngson was doing in this breakthrough film. In a December 27, 1957 column Crowther complained: "While we can thank Mr. Youngson, for another look at a few of the Mack Sennett and Hal Roach comedies of the Nineteen Twenties, we are not extravagantly in his debt for much else in this feature-length recapitulation of old memories. Mr. Youngson's narrative for the most part is impressionistic, sentimental and only film-deep, so to speak.

"Furthermore, the format of the film seems dictated merely by the limitations of the material available for this kind of thing, and not by any logical approach to the complex history of the early forms of cinema comedy. Mr. Youngson duly notes that it is now a thing of the past, but he never answers the question as to what has changed in our national psychology between then and now to bring about its demise.

"We get glimpses of Laurel and Hardy, Will Rogers, Carole Lombard, Jean Harlow, Ben Turpin, Harry Langdon, among others. But there is neither sight nor mention of W. C. Fields or Charlie Chaplin and no anticipation of the great comedy of the Thirties that was to follow. R.W.N."

John L. Scott, the reviewer for *Los Angeles Times*, March 7, 1958 wrote, "It's strictly a novelty offering but should prove interesting for those who would turn the clock back to 'remember when.' Younger movie fans will marvel at the 'corn' which 35 years ago convulsed film audiences the world over. Laurel and Hardy still provide the funniest gags and bring the loudest laughter, especially with their buildup comedy situation. They were indeed kings of fun in their time. A reel from *Two Tars* stars this unforgettable duo."

Fortunately, Laurel lived to see this film's salute to his comedy. Unfortunately, his partner Hardy had died on August 7, 1957, several months before *The Golden Age of Comedy* first opened in theaters.

Besides mentioning Rogers, Langdon, Turpin, Lombard, and Harlow, Scott acknowledges, "Others who ring the bell of remembrance include Daphne Pollard, Billy Bevan, Edgar Kennedy, Charlie Murray, Andy Clyde and Harry Gribbon."

A couple of years later, when *The Golden Age of Comedy* first appeared on television, it was "finally understood as a 'Cavalcade of Comedy.' " *Los Angeles Times* announced on December 16, 1963 that the film's broadcast was for the upcoming Sunday. The film "gets its first local showing at 7:30 p.m. on Channel 9. A cavalcade of comedy greats including The Keystone Kops, Will Rogers, Jean Harlow, Harry Langdon, Ben Turpin, Laurel and Hardy."

Weist and Ward Wilson offered the film's narration. MacGillivray: "Weist and Wilson were television and radio performers who divided Youngson's script between them. Wilson handled the lighter, wiseguy commentary; his brisk tenor was familiar from the *Can You Top This?* joke-telling panel show. The straight historical narration fell to Weist; his dignified baritone gave him a versatile range... "

The poignant narration that closes this first compilation of silent comedies is simple and it is effectively spoken over notes from Chopin's hauntingly nostalgic Étude in C Major, Opus 10, No. 3. Narrator: "The curtain lowers, the crowds depart, 'hail and farewell.' We will never see their like again. This is the end of a memory."

Robert Youngson's college days. Photo courtesy Jeanne Keyes Youngson.

The wedding of Jeanne Keyes and Robert Youngson. Photo courtesy Jeanne Keyes Youngson.

Thelma Ritter presents Academy Award. Photo courtesy Jeanne Keyes Youngson.

Jeanne Youngson. Photo courtesy Jeanne Keyes Youngson.

Two Cats of Hollywood

Not rival film beauties but two regular felines who found fame and fortunes in Hollywood and brought stardom by proxy to their mistress.

By JOAN TRACY

Puzzums and Ko-Fan, mongrel and aristocrat, well received in the cinema capital.

THIS is the story of the two most famous cats in Hollywood—and of their mistress, to whom they brought stardom by proxy. . . .

When Nadine Dennis was a little girl, she dreamed of the day when she would go to Hollywood and become a motion picture actress. A leading lady—and even, perhaps, a star!

It was not new, the dream. All over the world, in cities, in the country, in towns both large and small, other girls were living and dreaming the same sort of youthful, schoolgirl dreams. . . .

Hollywood was not big enough for all of them. Its starry firmament could not hold so many luminaries. . . . Nadine Dennis became just another one of the eager, striving girls who were pitting their youth and their glorious fresh beauty against the cold cruelty of the cameras—pitting their all and losing.

And Nadine Dennis might have been just like most of those others—lost and forgotten in the struggle. But because of a gentle, kindly deed, performed several years ago, she remains in Hollywood today, comfortably, happily, and with an income that is far from negligible. . . .

In 1926, during the cold grey hours of an October dawn, Nadine Dennis was awakened by wails and moans that came from somewhere in the fields near her window. At first she thought it was a trapped rat, but when she investigated she found a newly born kitten, half frozen from the cold, almost dead from starvation.

Picking up the poor, pitiful little animal, she carried it to her home and gave it into the keeping of her highly-prized Persian cat, which only a few days before had had kittens of her own.

Of high pedigree and royal lineage, the Persian frowned upon the mongrel kitten, and refused to allow it among her brood. But Nadine cared for it tenderly, feeding it from a bottle, until it was old enough to lap up milk by itself.

One of the Persian's kittens, Ko-Fan, began to play with the little waif,

Miss Nadine Dennis, with Puzzums, the kitten that repaid a debt.

which Nadine had named Puzzums, and the two cats became inseparable. In fact, Nadine could not leave them even to go to the studios in her daily search for work.

Occasionally her efforts were rewarded, and she obtained an obscure bit in some production. And while she was performing before the cameras, the two cats would sit on the sidelines, waiting quietly for her to finish.

And then, one day, an assistant director noticed them, and suggested that she show them to Mack Sennett, who could use them in his comedies.

At first she did not give the suggestion much consideration. After all, she was in Hollywood to get in pictures herself, not to train cats for movies. But the more she thought of it, the more she was inclined to give the idea a trial.

Acting on a hunch one day, she made the long trip out to the Sennett studio, where she was immediately offered a contract for Puzzums at the stupendous salary of $50 a week for the first week, graduating to $250 a week by the end of three years, the term of the agreement.

Today, Nadine Dennis has given up all intention of striving for stardom for herself. She has a comfortable home—a nice car—pretty clothes and pleasant friends. Her life is very full. She has no financial worries.

And her days are occupied in managing the business affairs of two of the most beautiful stars in Hollywood—The two cats!

The New Movie Magazine, July, 1932

Images courtesy of Scott MacGillivray.

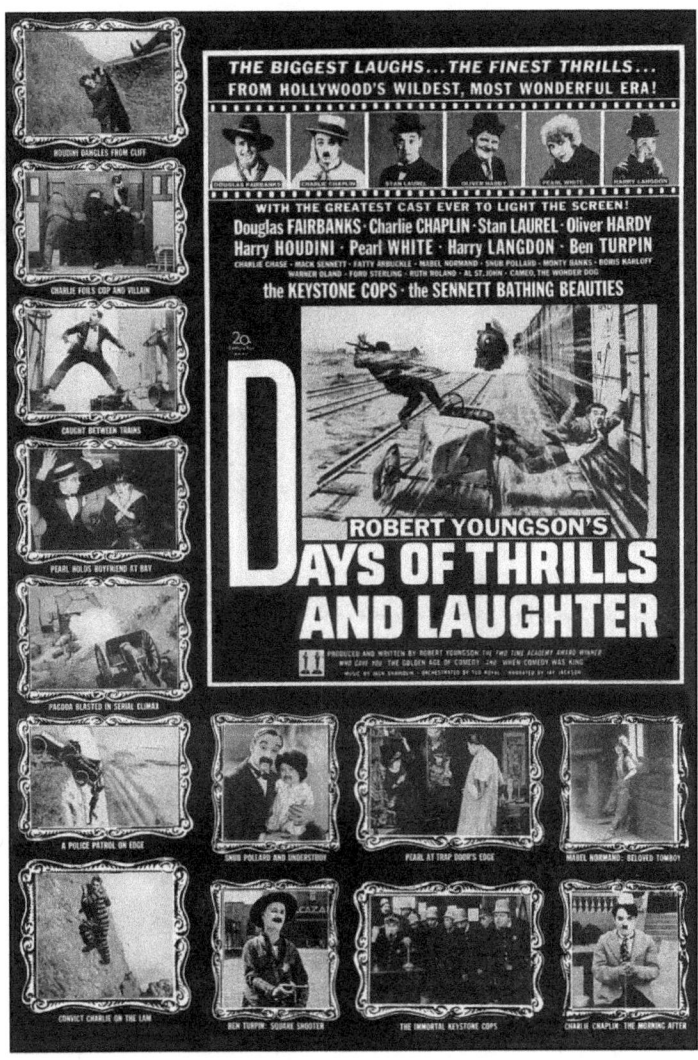

Image courtesy John McElwee.

Image courtesy of Scott MacGillivray.

Images courtesy of Scott MacGillivray.

Images courtesy of Scott MacGillivray.

Image Section • 79

Images courtesy of Scott MacGillivray.

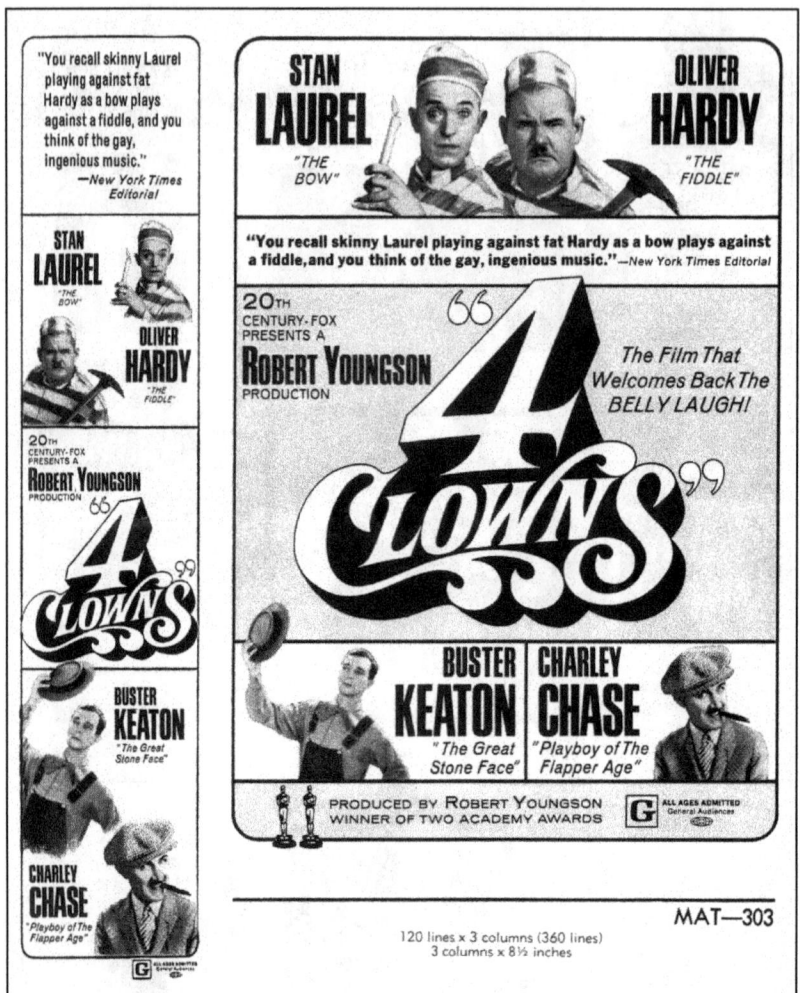

Images courtesy of Scott MacGillivray.

10

Bob Called It His Best

"It's a brilliant compilation of the best sight comedy from 1917 to 1928. He screened more than 2,500 reels of film for the best and funniest."

– Hedda Hopper on *When Comedy Was King*,
Los Angeles Times, May 24, 1960

A FEW MONTHS before his second compilation was released a surviving transcript of one of the Theodore Huff Memorial Film Society meetings reveals that the November 17, 1959 program presented one of Youngson's short films. Everson described it in the film notes as follows: "*Those Exciting Days* (Warner Bros, 1954, one reel), written and produced by Robert G. Youngson. We've shown quite a few of Bob Youngson's shorts in the past – both the condensations of silent features, and the reconstructions, via newsreel material, of specific eras and events from the teens and twenties. Generally speaking this latter classification was by far the more satisfactory of the two, the others tending to be vastly over-written, and *Those Exciting Days* is one of the best shorts of its type. The material is extremely well-chosen and occasionally over-sentimentalizes."

At another of the Theodore Huff Memorial Film Society meetings from which a transcript exists, the one on Tuesday, June 20, 1960, when his second compilation was in theaters, offered a potpourri of shorts including one by Youngson. According to the program notes, the schedule included, "*The Coming of the Auto* (Warners, 1953). Written and edited by Robert Youngson, ½ reel. This little segment was actually first compiled as a unit in a News Magazine for schools, then later incorporated into a theatrical short, *Looking at Life*. It's of interest to us since much of the footage comes from Warners' 1927 *The First Auto*, written by Darryl F. Zanuck and directed by Roy del Ruth. Its stars were Russell Simpson and Charles Ernst Mack (who, ironically was decapitated in an auto accident not long afterwards)."

Also included on that same program was another Youngson title: "*It Happened to You* (Warners, 1954) 2 reels, written directed by Robert G. Youngson. Although over-sentimentally written, this is a beautifully edited documentary coverage of America's participation in World War One. Reflecting the propaganda newsreels of the time, the stress is on jubilation, horse-play in the training camps, and the glory, excitement and patriotism of it all.

"Combat footage was relayed to the home front only in very small doses. Incidentally, this indisputable record of the nation's attitude at the time proves how well and accurately King Vidor re-created that attitude almost a decade later in *The Big Parade*. Some of the footage is extremely rare, and all of it is well put together. Incidentally, you'll notice a slight pop in the track between the shots of Mary Pickford and Doug selling bonds; initially Chaplin was there too, but the MPPA 'requested' that it be removed before release, it not being politic at that time to remind audiences that maybe Chaplin wasn't such a bad fellow after all."

Youngson's second compilation, *When Comedy Was King*, utilized Mack Sennett and Hal Roach material once again to continue the salute to the 1920s silent film slapstick comedians. This time Weist returned as the narrator.

The film begins with a narration over a sequence from Chase's short *Movie Night*: "Come chase along with Charley Chase and family across thirty years of time, back to a neighborhood theater of the 1920s. They called them 'Palaces of the Silent Drama' – though they were far from silent. There was always music. The only things missing were words; and from this very lack, there emerged a new art form. One that flourished then died. The art of the sight gag. Comedy to be seen not heard. Many believed it the greatest comedy of all. It was to be found on every screen of every theater every day. It made the 20s roar. We believe it will make you laugh as loudly as the audiences of so long ago. For the next 90 minutes, you will be part of a world a third of a century younger, 'When Comedy Was King.'"

Also over the credits, the narrator suggests, "As in the bygone days of vaudeville, if anything or anybody meets with your approval, we hope you will applaud. Somewhere ghosts may be listening."

A playful, fun mood is established early on via the credits of "Written and Produced by Robert Youngson" being moved in (with a cranked sound) upside down, and then sideways, before being correctly positioned.

As with his first film, Youngson continues to divide his film into sections with title cards. It begins with "The Good Old Days At Keystone," which includes Chaplin, Normand, Swain, Arbuckle, St. John, Wallace Beery, Swanson, and a dog named Keystone Teddy. The next section, "The Immortal Baby," offers us Langdon (along with Alice Day and Louise Carver). "Hal Roach: In and Out of the 1920s" offers two shorts, one with Pollard, and another with Erwin, Kennedy, Byron, and Garver.

Keaton gets his due in a section titled "The Great Stoneface." In "The Wacky World of Mack Sennett," the focus is on the chase and the comedy of surprise with the talents of Turpin, Bevan, Ruth Hiatt, Morgan, and the Keystone Kops. *When Comedy Was King* concludes with the section called "The Fiddle and the Bow," which focuses on Laurel & Hardy (with the assistance of James Finlayson).

When a scene with Chaplin and Normand is offered the narrator explains: "Like most of the Keystones, the Chaplin films were shot without a script, off the cuff. The actors ad-libbed their stuff as they went along. Scenes requiring split-second timing were made in this fashion, and they were rarely taken more than once. The reason for this method was economy, but the result sometimes was a brand of spontaneous fun unapproached since the passing of silent comedy."

Once again, as with *The Golden Age of Comedy*, this film offers a nostalgic view of the bygone past. Another thing that vanished is the prices. For instance, the narrator observes an eatery, saying, "Take a look at that sign from 40 years ago and weep!"

Another thing that has changed from the past regards what is acceptable as funny. The narrator, in reference to Chaplin, says, "In a time when the world's funny bone was far less touchy than it is now, Charlie has played the same solicitude for old men as he did for babes."

When Comedy Was King also acknowledges the sadness in the days to come to some of the great comedy players. On Chaplin, the narrator appreciates the innocence of the moment: "Chaplin's story of fabulous success and fabulous trouble was just beginning this bright September 45 years and two world wars ago." As regards Normand and Arbuckle the narrator says, "As Fatty and Mabel, they were beloved by the fans of 1916, and their appeal is still apparent in this little valentine of a comedy which has remained fresh and charming through the passing years.... Across the lives of madcap Mabel and jovial Fatty alike were to pass the shadows of scandal, ill fortune, and early death. But that too was the undreamed of future in these gay Keystone days."

In the excerpt from *Fatty and Mabel Adrift* (1916); as their bedroom fills with water, and their beds are afloat, Narrator: " 'My goodness,' wonders Fatty, 'did Mabel leave the bathtub running?' " Then Youngson makes a jab at today, asking: "Do the television-fed kids of today ever thrill as did the kids of old crouched down with eyes big in the magic darkness of the local bijou as scenes like this stagger their imagination?"

Again, as Youngson's compilations indicate, the silent comedies often give dogs the credit for saving the day. Narrator: "So Fatty and Mabel are rescued in this happiest of happy endings which proves that true love will always triumph thanks to man's best friend – the dog."

At the start, Youngson's narrator says, "Of the comedians who abounded in Comedy's Golden Age, a handful achieved greatness. And three of them, in the opinion of critics, were so completely original in their portrayals as to scale the heights of pure genius. You will meet all three in this picture – one is Chaplin."

In actuality, Youngson, as with others, may have recognized four great silent clowns here, if it had not been Harold Lloyd's choice to refuse anyone permission to use his films. This despite Youngson personally knowing and admiring Lloyd.

As regards scenes with Langdon, the film goes a bit further here than in the first compilation. Narrator: "Hollywood used to ask, who would replace Harry Langdon? In the quarter century since his passing, the answer has become clear: nobody."

Though Youngson included footage of Langdon in *The Golden Age of Comedy*, it is in *When Comedy Was King* that he gives us the reason for Langdon's creative demise. Narrator: "Langdon rose rapidly to stardom. Then at the height of his career, he turned in films directed by himself to a new strange offbeat type of comedy full of pathos and even despair. It was like a trumpeter reaching for a celestial high note somewhere beyond human range. Audiences stopped laughing. And the little fellow slid into oblivion...."

Youngson's overall importance in locating and compiling his productions is evident here when his narrator says, "In his three years with Sennett, Langdon created dozens of short masterpieces, most of which are forever lost. The film you are watching had already begun to decompose when it was copied barely in time to save it from extinction." Later some critics would not acknowledge this point as they denigrated Youngson for cutting up the shorts to make his compilations.

"No one better expressed the spirit of silent comedy than the hesitant, wistful Langdon, who as one critic put it, 'looked as if he wore diapers under his pants and had the face of a baby dope fiend.'"

Moving over to the Pollard short, we are treated to a superb comedy sequence that is full of inventive gadgets; including ones that allow the main character to pull strings to make breakfast while still in bed and get completely dressed in 30 seconds. Pollard's one-seat mini car moves by his directing a large magnet in the direction of other cars. Narrator: "This inventive picture entitled *It's A Gift*, represented Pollard's finest moment, for soon new stars would arise on the Roach lot and Snub began the long spiral down. But today, all too few remember the brash little fellow with a Kaiser Wilhelm moustache worn upside down."

There are a number of other superior comedy excerpts in *When Comedy Was King*. Narrator: "...Buster Keaton: The third of the three great and completely original comedy talents to rise in splendor during comedy's golden years. Chaplin was the tramp. Langdon was the baby, Keaton was the Great Stoneface around whose impassive figure mad havoc roared like debris around the dead eye of a hurricane.

"...From Mark Twain to Will Rogers, America has had many dry wits whose humor sprang from words. Buster Keaton remains it's only dry visual comedian."

Youngson's passionate love of the 1920s comedies is obvious in all of his compilations. There is no getting away from his appreciation of immense amount of visual wit packed into those films. He directly suggests his own disappointment with his sparse comedy of the late 1950s in his section on Sennett. There the narrator concludes: "And so it is that Ben Turpin bows out of our picture, obeying a prime rule of silent screen comedians: 'Exit running.' Thirty years later, Mack Sennett, the old master himself, was to look back at his wacky world of old and wonder, 'What has happened to laughter? There used to be so much of it.'"

When Comedy Was King includes Chaplin in *The Masquerader* (1914), *His Trysting Place* (1914), and *Gentlemen of Nerve* (1914). There is Swanson and Wallace Beery in *Teddy at the Throttle* (1917); Langdon in *The First 100 Years* (1924); Kennedy in *A Pair of Tights* (1929); Turpin in *Yukon Jake* (1924); Bevan in *Wall Street Blues* (1924), *Super-Hooper-Dyne Lizzies* (1925), *The Lion's Whiskers* (1925), and *Wandering Willies* (1926);

and Laurel & Hardy in *Big Business* (1929). Also seen here is Mack Swain, Conklin, and Al [Fuzzy] St. John.

One of the earliest ads for *When Comedy Was King* appeared in *New York Times* on March 27, 1960. It utilizes artwork of the cast drawn on a long winding line, including Chaplin, Laurel and Hardy, Arbuckle, the Keystone Kops, etc.

It reads, "THE ALL-TIME GREATEST COMEDY CAST! IN THE ALL-TIME FUNNIEST COMEDY FILM! HERE'S A DREAM COME TRUE – THE MOST WONDERFUL COMEDIANS THE SCREEN HAS KNOWN IN THEIR BEST MOVIE MOMENTS – A FABULOUS FEATURE OF NOTHING BUT BELLY LAUGHS!"

The ad lists the cast of Chaplin, Laurel & Hardy, Keaton, Langdon, Turpin, Arbuckle, Beery, Swanson, Normand, The Keystone Kops, Chase, Kennedy, The Sennett Girls, Conklin, and Clyde.

The *Los Angeles Times* ad on the same day pictured just six drawings (Laurel, Hardy, Chaplin, Turpin, Keaton and Langdon). It offered: "EVERYBODY LOVES TO LAUGH" and 'HERE'S A FILM THE ENTIRE FAMILY WILL ENJOY – AND TALK ABOUT FOR MONTHS"

In "Silent Comedies Yielding 3D Film," *New York Times*, April 2, 1960, Howard Thompson reported, "Robert Youngson is not a filmmaker to rest on his laurels, past or present. At the moment, critical laurels are crowning the small Sixty-eighth Street Playhouse on Third Avenue, where last Wednesday Mr. Youngson's *When Comedy Was King* topped the forty-five-year-old theatre's record for opening-day grosses. Meanwhile the writer-producer disclosed yesterday that in about three months he will put finishing touches to still another silent-film compilation, *Days of Thrills and Laughter*.

"Mr. Youngson calls the forthcoming feature, his third culled from silent comedy footage, a 'cosmic thriller, representing over a year's inspection of pictures from a bygone era and focusing on the great comedy names of the past and one thing that's still loved and treasured the world over the old-time belly-laugh.'

"As a successful designer of commercial packages documenting 'the good old days,' Mr. Youngson traces his interest back to a 'childhood hobby – moviegoing.'

"Although pleased with the Twentieth Century-Fox sponsorship of his current comedy feature, Mr. Youngson shies away from the business details at 37 East Forty-Ninth Street. 'I'm happiest over at Park Ridge, N.J.,' he says, 'where it's safer to look at combustible old nitrate film, not all of it good, selecting from about 2,500 reels for a new feature. To me it's worth all the effort, and apparently the public agrees.'"

On the day after it opened (March 30, 1960), in New York City's Sixty-eighth Playhouse, *New York Times* critic called the film, "this flavorsome collection." Crowther: "The wonderful joy that surged in movies – in some movies, anyhow – back in the era of silent pictures and the heyday of the famous screen clowns surges again for fitful stretches in *When Comedy Was King*.... It is a charmingly simple memory album that Mr. Youngson has compiled and equipped with an excellent musical sound track and a mildly nostalgic narration. His somewhat historical annotations, spoken by Weist, are helpful, if one cares to listen, but are not essential to full enjoyment.

"No academic preparation is required to appreciate the fun in the kind of pantomimic madness that the old silent comedians indulged. Theirs was a world of wild extensions of all the embarrassments and agonies of life, even to death and taxes, heaped on the comic victims' heads. The comics themselves were the fall guys, only occasionally coming out on top. The villains were all the representations of authority and brutality. Even today, despite television and the preponderance of the wisecrack and gag, their dilemmas are as apt and fresh as ever. Here's a toast to this sort of comedy!"

In a follow-up article entitled "Change in Comedy" (*New York Times*, April 3, 1960), Crowther offered a comparison of *When Comedy Was King* alongside another new comedy release, *Please Don't Eat the Daisies*. Crowther: "And yet, of the two, for all the crudeness and sketchiness of the first – for all its titanic bumptiousness and pretense in a glaringly obsolete style – we found it so much more amusing than the second, the modern comedy, that it fuzzes our power of reasoning to think on what has been lost – and why?"

He noted that the simplification that sound killed slapstick comedy is untrue, as "some great 'sight' comedians such as Laurel and Hardy and the Marx Brothers have performed remarkably well in talking films.... The slapstick techniques, exaggeration and the comic felicities of pantomime are not excluded by sound in motion pictures. They have been ruled out by other things.

"But, unfortunately, there are no young comedians schooled as those silent comics were, and the likelihood of any being developed grows more and more remote every day. We were talking recently to Robert Youngson, who assembled *When Comedy Was King* and fixed it up with a narration (more nostalgic than historically reliable) and a musical score. He made an astute observation: slapstick comedians must be young men. Chaplin or Keaton are pathetic when they make passes in their old style today."

According to Crowther, current comedies are "amiable, usually harmless ventures in the realm of wise-crack farce, funny enough by current standards (television standards, that is), but almost feeble by comparison with the energetic stuff of the old clowns."

Crowther concluded, "Considering the pallid quality of most screen comedy these days, it is gladdening but saddening, we must tell you, to look at *When Comedy Was King.*"

One of the few interviews given by Youngson happened on Sunday April 17, 1960 from 8 to 8:45 p.m. Gideon Bachmann interviewed him on WBAI-FM's *The Film Art*. The radio show's topic was "Comedy Then and Now: Silent vs. Sound."

Hopper, *Los Angeles Times*, May 17, 1960: "If you're looking for good clean comedy by such as Buster Keaton, Laurel and Hardy, Harry Langdon, Ben Turpin, Mabel Normand, etc., go and see *When Comedy Was King*... It's bringing laughter back into the theaters and taking the sour taste of degradation and sex pictures out of your mouth."

Los Angeles Times, May 20, 1960, Geoffrey Warren observed: "The youngsters who wept bucketfuls of tears of laughter at the old silent comedies and who now recount these wonders to their grandchildren need no longer wonder if they would still be funny today. To the question posed the answer is yes, and if they want to see for themselves they can find satisfaction in a two-hour visit to the Hollywood Vogue Theater where an eight reel anthology of some of the best is showing under the title of *When Comedy Was King*.

"Considered one of the greatest, Harry Langdon seems to have been lost at the end of his day. One can see why he was appreciated, but he doesn't come through particularly well today. Fatty Arbuckle and Mabel Normand still have considerable appeal, and Gloria Swanson and Wallace Beery, as heroine and villain, with Keystone Teddy, were and still are entertaining. The famous Keystone Kops, Ben Turpin, Charlie Chase, Edgar Kennedy, Stuart Erwin, Andy Clyde and Chester Conklin have a comedy magic that should be good for years to come. Snub Pollard, Al St. John, Bobby Vernon are others who wear remarkably well."

This compilation concluded with Laurel & Hardy selling Christmas trees from their *Big Business* short. Warren: "...this gem begins with disappointment, follows with misunderstanding, confusion, temper, anger, vengeance, retribution and finally chaos as Laurel and Hardy take Finlayson's house apart while he disassembles their Model T. It's paralyzing. This adventure into Hollywood's comedy past was ably produced by Robert Youngson, who also wrote the excellent narration."

There are many times when Youngson through his narrator reveals his intense love and longing for the 1920s. One particular aspect from the period that is referred to in *When Comedy Was King* is the clothing of the day. In the Garvin short, the narrator reminds us: "We've had short skirts since then but never had skirts so delightfully short, nor girls so cute as in the breezy 20s."

MacGillivray reported that the domestic earnings were $438,000, and internationally it was nearly double that at $834.000. He noted that John McElwee indicated a net profit $115,000 due to costs associated with post-production and publicity. According to McElwee, "Costs for compiling the features were minimal, but expenses incurred with prints, advertising, and distribution added up, much in the same way as they would for any A feature handled by Fox."

When VidAmerica released the film on videotape for $39.95, *New York Times*, March 15, 1987, Walter Goodman noted, "Robert Youngson's *When Comedy Was King* begins with Charley Chase causing commotion in a movie theater, zips into early and choice Chaplin, and follows up nonstop with keen Keaton, the funniest and most havoc-wrecking short Laurel and Hardy ever made, a side-splitting, clothes-splatting skit about the troubles you can get into trying to eat an ice-cream cone, not to mention wild chases, pies in faces, and more hijinks and pratfalls than you can shake a stick at – and plenty of sticks are shaken here."

Everson told MacGillivray: "He felt that *When Comedy Was King* was the best. He felt it was the most polished, and was introducing people like Keaton and the best of Laurel & Hardy to an audience that otherwise wouldn't have seen them. So he was very satisfied with that one."

As with his first compilation, Youngson closes *When Comedy Was King* with another poignant narration intoned over notes from Chopin's Étude in C. Major, Opus 10, No. 3. Narrator: "Now the fiddle and the bow can play no more. Time has ended the concert. The world is beginning to realize how much it loved fat Oliver and skinny Stan. So ends our visit to the era of the great silent clowns who mass produced laughter and sold happiness, and who passed into oblivion just before the years when the world needed them most."

11

With Added Thrills

"If Robert Youngson isn't the best producer 20th Century-Fox has, it is only because he is the best reproducer."

– Philip K. Scheuer on *Days of Thrills and Laughter*, *Los Angeles Times*, May 31, 1961

IN HIS THIRD COMPILATION, Youngson offered more than just the usually funny comedy moments from Langdon, Laurel & Hardy, Pollard, Turpin et al. He provided thrills from Douglas Fairbanks, serial stars such as Pearl White, Ruth Roland, Warner Oland, Boris Karloff and Harry Houdini, and others.

MacGillivray: "Youngson may have hoped that this new combination would popularize silent-screen adventure, as his other features had revived silent comedy. It didn't work out that way. The film was less relevant to the 1961 public; the comic parts were timeless, but the straight footage dated badly." In comparison to his second compilation, MacGillivray reported, "*Days of Thrills and Laughter* did about two-thirds the business of *When Comedy Was King* ($291,000 domestic gross, $557,000 international)."

A year before its release, Thompson reported that in Youngson's next compilation, "After a section on the American emergence of the Keystone comedies and two Chaplin portions will come a one-reel condensation of *Wild and Woolly*, an early Douglas Fairbanks effort showing the dashing adventurer as a tenderfoot braving the rigors of the Old West.... However, Mr. Youngson considers the highlight a 'review of serial climaxes,' featuring Walter Miller, Boris Karloff, Jacqueline Logan and, of course, the two serial queens, Pearl White and Ruth Roland."

The New York Times announced Youngson's third feature when it reported on November 1, 1960: "*Days of Thrills and Laughter*, Robert Youngson's compilation of scenes from silent serials, including Pearl White's *Perils of Pauline*, will be distributed next spring by Twentieth Century-Fox. The new anthology type of feature follows a similar format to the producer's *The Golden Age of Comedy* and *When Comedy Was King*."

A *New York Times* clip announced the film would begin screenings on March 23, 1961 at the 68th Street Playhouse, and described it as "a compilation of key sequences by silent screen performers."

Everson told MacGillivray: "In *Days of Thrills and Laughter*, what he used was public-domain stuff that he could find, like the Houdini, Douglas Fairbanks and serial material, most of which he found here in New York. It certainly wasn't the Grade-A stuff that he really wanted."

On March 19, 1961, a *New York Times* ad for the film read, "THE MOST EXCITING EPISODES FROM THE GREAT THRILLERS… THE HIGHLIGHT MOMENTS FROM THE IMMORTAL COMEDIES… ALL TOGETHER IN THE FUN FILM OF THE YEAR!" The names billed are listed in the ad in no particular order it seems, though they are all in capital letters running down the side of the ad: "DOUGLAS FAIRBANKS, CHARLIE CHAPLIN STAN LAUREL, OLIVER HARDY, HOUDINI, PEARL WHITE, HARRY LANGDON, CHARLIE CHASE, MACK SENNETT, FATTY ARBUCKLE, BEN TURPIN, BORIS KARLOFF, MONTY BANKS, WARNER OLAND, FORD STERLING, RUTH ROLAND, AL ST. JOHN, CAMEO the Wonder Dog.

In the center of the ad is, "Produced and Written by ROBERT YOUNGSON the TWO-TIME ACADEMY AWARD WINNER who gave you 'THE GOLDEN AGE OF COMEDY' and 'WHEN COMEDY WAS KING.' " Below that is the addition to the billed stars: "PLUS THE KEYSTONE KOPS, THE SENNETT BATHING BEAUTIES."

Two days later a *New York Times* article appeared announcing that the film would open on that day at a first-run theater; namely, New York City's 68th Street Playhouse. The ad from that paper noted: "20 OF THE FUNNIEST, MOST DARING STARS EVER ON THE SCREEN!" and "EVERY MOMENT… A LAUGH, A THRILL… FROM THE OPENING TITLE UNTIL THE SCREEN FLASHES 'THE END' "

Weiler, *New York Times*, March 22, 1961, observed, "By its very nature this makes an uneven compilation but it is nevertheless, an urbane, yet uncondescending peep into the past that is a reminder of the invention and artistry of the uninhibited moviemakers of the silent era.

"A viewer whose experience dates back to Sennett-Chaplin chapters of film history of more than forty years ago may not find this package entirely revelatory. But time does dim memory, and another look at Chaplin skittering around corners fleeing from prison guards in *The Adventurer* or blithely exposing his comic genius as the drunk in *The Cure* will make for a greater appreciation of his authentically stupendous talent, as well as despair for the absence of such these days.

"The younger set, exposed to cliché-ridden and generally dubious comedy of the present, undoubtedly will savor it, too, judging by the reaction of junior citizens in attendance yesterday. If Mr. Youngson's meticulous compilation leaves an observer with a feeling that this is merely a surface view and yearning for the originals, entire and whole, it has accomplished its purpose.

"*Days of Thrills and Laughter* does provide enough of each of these ingredients to prove that pioneer pictures, illogical and inane though they might have been, did move without the benefit of palaver and gave the customers more than a modicum of action, adventure and laughs."

The March 24, 1961, *New York Times* ad for the film provided some of the reviewers' comments. It reads:

> 'TRULY FUNNY! A reminder of the invention and artistry of uninhibited moviemakers! Makes for a greater appreciation of Chaplin's authentically stupendous talent.' – *N.Y. Times*
>
> 'A CINEMA CLASSIC! Some of the funniest episodes ever committed to film by men who were masters of their trade! Outlandishly hilarious! Priceless!' – *N.Y. Mirror*
>
> 'Movies that really move! Great Fun! A nostalgic treat!' – *N.Y. Daily News*
>
> 'A good time is had by all! Pure classics! Gales of laughter!' – *N.Y. Post*
>
> 'Most hilarious of Robert Youngson's compilations! A carnival of nostalgia! An experience in comedy!' – *N.Y. World-Telegram*."

Above the newspaper reviews the ad declared: "COVETED ANNUAL 'PAGE ONE' AWARD For outstanding achievement in motion pictures to ROBERT YOUNGSON 'For bringing back to the screen the excitement of what movies used to be' in DAYS OF THRILLS AND LAUGHTER."

With just two Youngson compilations since his breakthrough, Crowther is seemingly a fan. *New York Times*, March 26, 1961: "Back when the screen was silent, many directors would start a picture with no more than a rough idea, then cook up a story and the business as they went along. It was a whimsical and stimulating practice, known colloquially as 'shooting off the cuff.'

"That was all right for silent pictures, especially slapstick comedies, which got a lot of their explosive characteristics from the spontaneous invention of mad sight gags. (If you want to see how, incidentally, and have a jolly time to boot, go to see Robert Youngson's third anthology of old time comedies… "

In *"Thrills, Laughter* Whirlwind of Fun," *Los Angeles Times*, May 31, 1961, Scheur described Youngson's latest release as "the best 93 minutes of cinema in town. Did the laughter come easier then? If you had sat among the crowded (I was delighted to note) audience at the Vogue Monday night and listened to the unforced gales of hilarity that filled the festive air, you would have realized that the people haven't changed as much as the pictures have. If Robert Youngson isn't the best producer 20th Century-Fox has, it is only because he is the best reproducer."

MacGillivray: "Bill Everson confirmed Youngson's one-man bandwagon style: 'He loved the sense of being a total producer with all the power it brought, and he had a tremendous ego. [He supervised] absolutely *everything*, and designed all the ads and the copy for the pressbooks. He was very proud of the fact that he was an Academy Award winner and nominee for other films, and always made sure that byline was in all the ads.'"

Days of Thrills and Laughter serves as an enjoyable tribute to Hollywood's silent movies featuring classic action and comedy scenes. The film begins with a French silent, *The Bath Chair Man* (1904), which features a city chase involving three people plus a man taking a bath in a rolling chair. Another clip shows bathing beauties of 1916 playing on the beach and in an indoor pool.

Other excerpts include scenes of Pollard in *The Movies* (1922), *Spot Cash* (1921), *Blow 'em Up* (1922), *The Joy Riders* (1921), and *Late Lodgers* (1921). Also seen is Normand in *Mabel's Dramatic Career* (1913); The

Keystone Cops in *Her Torpedoed Love* (1917); Chaplin in *The Adventurer* (1917), and *The Cure* (1916). There is Fairbanks Sr. in *Wild and Woolly* (1917); Bevan in *Whispering Whiskers* (1926); Turpin in *Home Made Movies* (1922), and *Asleep at the Switch* (1923); Hardy in *The Hobo* (1917), and *Say It with Babies* (1926); Laurel in *Kill or Cure* (1923); Langdon in *All Night Long* (1924); and Arthur Stone in *Sherlock Sleuth* (1925).

A number of clips from silent serials are included; such as Houdini in *The Master Mystery* (1919), and *The Man from Beyond* (1922); White in *The Lightning Raider* (1919), and *The Perils of Pauline* (1914); Roland in *The Tiger's Tail* (1919) and *The Timber Queen* (1922). Also seen is Walter Miller and Karloff in *King of the Kongo* (1929); Gladys McConnell in *The Fire Detective* (1929); Allene Ray in *The Man Without a Face* (1928), and *The Yellow Cameo* (1928); Ralph Kellard in *The Shielding Shadow* (1916); Monty Banks in *Play Safe* (1927); and Chase in *Accidental Accidents* (1924).

Other stars include Cameo the Wonder Dog, Dixie Chene, Al Christie, Clyde, Virginia Fox, Bud Jamison, Eddie Lyons, Lee Moran, Marie Mosquini, Billie Rhodes, Sennett, Al [Fuzzy] St. John, Ford Sterling, Billy West, Crane Wilbur, Leo Willis, and Noah Young.

Days of Thrills and Laughter had Jay Jackson as the narrator. Jackson would eventually narrate five of the eight films.

The film opens to the strains of Chopin's Étude in C Major, Opus 10, No. 3. What is different this time is that Youngson brings us a fine banjo arrangement of the tune. The narrator opens saying, "*Days of Thrills and Laughter* proudly presents the first double feature titles, especially designed for the members of our audience who are tired of reading credits. If you are one of those, watch the screen being formed on the left and rough it with Snub Pollard in that day long past when motion picture theaters were called nickelodeons. For moviegoers who feel no film is complete without them, the usual credit titles will unfold on the right."

Youngson's penchant for bringing the audience totally into the 1920s world of comedy even begins with the opening credits of *Days of Thrills and Laughter*. With the background score composed and conducted by Jack Shaindlin, the title credits of Shaindlin's name is enlarged, with the narrator saying, "Hold it. O.K., bring up that name. That's enough. Sorry folks, it's in his contract."

When the credit titles reach "Produced and Written by Robert Youngson," Bob's name is enlarged and spun around until it fills the screen, and then it is shrunk until it disappears. The accompanying narration is: "Hold it. What a showoff. Take Youngson down. All the way down. Let's keep this movie moving." Clearly putting this gag in the opening of the film proves that his sense of humor extends to even being self-deprecating.

With the film's opening credits finished, the comedy short ends, flashing "The End" on the screen. Then a new title card reads "The Beginning." Narrator: "The beginning was some seventy years ago when man learned to imprison time and motion on film. With hand-cranked cameras and sun for lighting, movie pioneers concocted the first photoplays and discovered that the surest way to please an audience was to make it laugh. The best of the early comedies came from France where geniuses like Méliès and Zecca explored the camera's endless possibilities."

What is perfectly appropriate is how Youngson breaks the subject into parts, and informs his audience. Narrator: "Mack Sennett is remembered for two contributions to the very lively art of the motion picture. One, the Keystone Kops whose chases were symphonies in misguided motion." What follows is a collection of madcap chases.

Narrator: "A second unforgettable contribution, the Mack Sennett Bathing Beauties. Their saucy rags launched the bathing suit revolution that's snowballing down the years has led from the Mother Hubbard to the bikini." We are shown scenes from various films featuring the Sennett girls.

After that, we see a shot of kids all running in the street towards the camera. The scene is from Spring Valley, New York traveling cinematographers who are photographing kids trek to holiday movie matinee. Narrator: "Oh, to be a kid again on a long ago Saturday afternoon racing to the local bijou to see the little man who had came up from Keystone to become the most popular comedian anywhere anytime." The title that appears over the kids is "The Kid From Keystone." Of course, this refers to Chaplin.

Next up is "The Dashing American," a salute to Douglas Fairbanks. Doug plays a rich New Yorker bent on seeing the Old West, but in his mind the bygone West of the 1880s. Doug's father, a railroad tycoon, sends for his son, the narrator oddly remarks: "In this bygone era, as you can plainly see, America was as not as yet plagued by a servant problem."

"Comedy's Golden Twenties" focuses on Sennett's competitor Roach, providing laughs from Pollard, St. John, Laurel, Hardy, and Turpin. In addition, it includes Langdon in a Sennett short, Arthur Stone/Martha Sleeper and the studio lion.

"The Thrillers" includes Houdini, serial stars Pearl White, Warner Oland, Ruth Roland, Walter Miller, and Boris Karloff.

"Thrills and Laughter" combined the two in a blend by giving us a large portion of a Monty Banks short.

"Three for the Road" offered two more Pollard shorts and closed with Chase.

Days of Thrills and Laughter ended sadly with the banjo playing the final haunting notes of the familiar Chopin tune. Narrator: "These then were the Days of Thrills and Laughter. A time so long past that the youngest members of this departing audience are today in their fifties. As for the laugh makers and thrill makers, they too have vanished leaving behind no successors but only moving shadows. So the crowds depart, the show is over. And alas dear friends, our little show is over too."

12

The Fun Continues

"*[30 Years of Fun]* was obviously designed for audiences that have never seen old movies.... They may find it a riot just to see actors in old-fashioned clothes making jerky gestures on a speeded-up strip of film."

– Eugene Archer, *New York Times*,
December 26, 1963

FOR HIS FOURTH COMPILATION, Youngson went a step further when he added footage taken from silent newsreels along with composing an overly sentimental song to express his heart-felt feelings regarding the silent comedies. Youngson's song, entitled, "Bring Back The Laughter," is heard while audiences see the credits roll over newsreel footage. Orchestrated by Bernard Green and Milton Weinstein and conducted by Green, the latter also sang the song using a pseudonym. The title credits read, "Words by Robert Youngson, Sung by Bernie Knee."

MacGillivray aptly noted, "It was a slow slushy hymn to days of yore... The ballad of Robert Youngson didn't help the picture."

Although the words played over comedy clips do not Mickey Mouse the lyrics, nor are they irrelevant, the music seems so dated and lacking energy. The somewhat dirge-like tune definitely lacks the nostalgic and longing quality of Chopin's Étude in C Major, Op. 10, No. 3. Perhaps Youngson should have written words to Chopin's music instead as that most effectively conveyed the correct mood of longing as in the previous compilations.

Nevertheless, here are the sappy lyrics to Youngson's tune:

"Bring back the laughter that we used to know,
When the movies were young, so long, long ago.
Bring back the great clowns, so sad, so absurd,
As they made millions laugh, never singing a word.
Bring back the proud cop, the pie in the face,
The villain whose vanquished in fiendish disgrace.
The chill of September has come all too soon,
Through yesterday's magic, once more make it June.
Bring back the laughter we used to know,
And the dark at the bijou, so long, long ago.
Bring back the flappers so useless and yet,
With a sweet sign of beauty, we can never forget.
Bring back the wild chase that wrecked a whole town,
A bashful hick hero with pants falling down.
The chill of September has come all too soon.
Through yesterday's magic, once more make it June."

Jeanne told MacGillivray: "He was very talented. I wouldn't say that he was a frustrated full-time composer, but he could do all these things."

The 1963 release, *30 Years of Fun*, included newsreel footage. There is a steam train on elevated tracks in New York City, footage from an Easter Parade; employees leaving the French film factory of the Lumière Brothers; and French soldiers in an army camp. Theodore Roosevelt is shown as a soldier with the Rough Riders, and giving a speech to women seeking the vote. The Wright Brothers in one of their airplanes; various French films circa 1904-1906; San Francisco before and after the earthquake of 1906; early automobiles; the end of World War One; Prohibition; behind the scenes in Hollywood; 1920s dance marathons; and a series of chases.

One of the finds that Youngson brings to viewers is a film that had been considered long lost: Laurel's first pairing with Hardy in a 1921 short entitled *Lucky Dog*. We also see Hardy alone in the 1927 short *Why Girls Say No*.

The compilation offers us Chaplin in *The Rink* (1916), *The Floorwalker* (1916), *The Pawnshop* (1916), and *Easy Street* (1917); Pollard in *The Jail Bird* (1921) and *Own Your Home* (1921). There is Irving Bacon in *Hurry Doctor* (1925) and *Whispering Whiskers* (1924); Langdon in *Feet of Mud* (1924) and *Smile Please* (1924); Bevan in *Whispering Whiskers* (1924); *Skinners in Silk* (1925); *One Cylinder Love* (1923); *The Golf Nut* (1927); and *The Best Man* (1928).

Chase is seen in *Publicity Pays* (1924), *Big Red Riding Hood* (1925), and *Bromo and Juliet* (1926); Syd Chaplin in *A Submarine Pirate* (1915); Fairbanks [Sr.] and Mary Pickford in footage from a World War One Liberty Bond campaign; Keaton in *The Balloonatic* (1923) and *Daydreams* (1922); and Carter DeHaven and his wife Flora Parker DeHaven in *Christmas* (1922).

On March 6, 1963, the *Los Angeles Times* reported that Youngson planned to appear on the children's TV show *Discovery '63* at 4:30 p.m. on Channel 7. The news clip noted, "The world of the great silent comedians is on tap today. Robert Youngson, collector of old films, will show and discuss rare old films featuring Buster Keaton, Charlie Chaplin and the Keystone Kops." This seems to be the only time that Youngson received major newspaper attention announcing a planned television appearance.

Eugene Archer, *New York Times*, brought attention to a problem with Youngson's *30 Years of Fun*: "More discriminating customers will find less cause for rejoicing… In fact, they may well be annoyed by the way the producer has treated some of their vintage favorites. For, by projecting the clips on a modern wide screen, Mr. Youngson has merely chopped the tops and bottoms off the images, with highly unsatisfactory results.

"…As if this were not enough, the producer has attempted to improve the comedy by increasing the speed of projection. The result, with actors scrambling around at twice their intended pace, does little damage to some of the minor comedians included in the footage here, but it destroys the effect of the subtle timing of the incomparable Chaplin… Still, ruined Chaplin is better than none – and the same may be said for Buster Keaton."

Walter Brecher from New York City sent a letter to the Screen Editor of the *New York Times*, published in the January 5, 1964 issue defending Youngson's fourth film compilation.

Brecher: "With regard to Eugene Archer's daily review of *Thirty Years of Fun* (December 26, 1963) may I enter a few remarks in defense of producer Robert Youngson. Please don't blame him for the fact that 'modern wide-screen' projection has chopped the tops and bottoms off the images. The fault lies with the inertia of the average exhibitor, who has committed himself to the wide-screen projection pattern.

"A few theaters, including the 68th Street Playhouse, have enough respect for Mr. Youngson's collection of old films to restore their projection equipment to the original aspect ratio in which this antique film was shot. Heads and feet are not left to the imagination, and, indeed, the reappearance of the old familiar shape, which is almost square, helps even further to recapture the antique flavor of his classics."

Some more publicity came his way when on Friday, September 4, 1964, at 2:30 – 3 p.m., Youngson discussed movie-making with Duncan MacDonald on WQXR radio's *Observation Point*. And then later that month, on September 23, 1964 from 12:10 – 1:55 p.m., Candy Jones interviewed Youngson and Jack Benny on WNBC radio.

13

The Sound Disappointment

"Great as those sound comedies were, they didn't lend themselves to excerpting. A lot of that material just didn't cut down out of context. [Youngson] was an absolute genius at getting the real nuggets out of the silent stuff, but I think the sound tended to drag."

– Everson told MacGillivray on
M-G-M's Big Parade of Comedy

WITH YOUNGSON'S FAME now assured, M-G-M invited the development of his next film by giving him complete access to their vaults. The result of this agreement resulted in two films.

His fifth compilation, released in 1964, had its narration done by radio and film actor Les Tremayne. MacGillivray: "Youngson handed him another of his challenging scripts, filled with equal doses of saccharine sentiment and hokey humor. Tremayne's sensitive delivery made the overwritten parts bearable and the tongue-in-cheek parts amusing."

The editor and Youngson's personal assistant Al Dahlem now got billing as Associate Producer. As regards a *Variety* reviewer of *M-G-M's Big Parade of Comedy*, MacGillivray: "The reviewer gave special credit to Jeanne Keyes 'as research supervisor, a mammoth undertaking well executed.' Mrs. Youngson modestly downplays her research duties: 'I used to go to the New York Public Library and check out copyrights.'"

Jeanne told MacGillivray that she received credit in the films under her maiden name because Bob, "was also billing his father [as production manager], and he didn't want to have too many Youngsons. He thought it was tacky."

Youngson receives credit for writing the lyrics for the songs offered in this compilation: "Jean, Oh Jean" (Bernard Green; Youngson); "Marie" (Green; Youngson); and "Big Parade of Comedy March" (Green; Youngson).

The sound comedies from Metro-Goldwyn-Mayer Studios were in the spotlight here. The highlights included various vintage scenes re-edited for the studio's 1930s short subjects, including *Cooky Movies* and *Pete Smith Specialties*; and shots of the various movie studios. The star clips included Larry Semon in *Kid Speed* (1924) and *The Cloudhopper* (1925); John Gilbert in *Show People* (1928); Joan Crawford in an MGM promotional film and *The Boob* (1926); Marion Davies in *The Red Mill* (1927) and *Show People* (1928); Karl Dane, George K. Arthur, and Polly Moran in *China Bound* (1929); George K. Arthur and Marceline Day in *Detectives* (1928); Keaton in *The Cameraman* (1928); and Chaplin in *Show People* (1928).

There are clips of Jimmy Durante in *Hollywood Party* (1934); Marie Dressler in *Reducing* (1931) and *Tugboat Annie* (1933); Harlow in *Hold Your Man* (1933), *Bombshell* (1933), *Girl from Missouri* (1934), *Suzy* (1936), *Personal Property* (1937), *Libeled Lady* (1936), and *Dinner at Eight* (1933); Lombard in *The Gay Bride* (1934); The Three Stooges in *Hollywood Party* (1934); and W.C. Fields in *David Copperfield* (1935).

There is the egg-breaking scene from Laurel & Hardy in *Hollywood Party* (1934) and a dance routine from *Bonnie Scotland* (1935). MacGillivray noted, "Youngson actually *improved* the dance by erasing the repetitive band music and recording a jaunty medley of Scottish airs instead."

Youngson also presented Clark Gable in *Too Hot to Handle* (1938); Katharine Hepburn and Cary Grant in *The Philadelphia Story* (1940); and Robert Benchley in *That Inferior Feeling* (1940), *How to Read* (1938), and *A Night at the Movies* (1937).

There is some attention given to the *Thin Man* series with William Powell, Myrna Loy, and Asta (a dog); Powell and Gail Patrick in *Love Crazy* (1941); Abbott & Costello in *Rio Rita* (1942); Lucille Ball in *Meet the People* (1944); Red Skelton in *A Southern Yankee* (1948); Greta Garbo in *Ninotchka* (1939) and *Two-Faced Woman* (1941); The Marx Brothers in *Go West* (1940); and Dave O'Brien in a parade of *Pete Smith Specialties* clips.

Scheuer, *Los Angeles Times*, August 30, 1963 reported, "From Robert Benchley to Greta Garbo – with a couple of dozen other stars thrown in.

That's the recipe for *Big Parade of Comedy*, which documentary expert Robert Youngson (*When Comedy Was King, 30 Years of Fun*) will whip together from the archives of MGM… The mélange should be ready to meld by November."

Crowther's column on September 4, 1964 (*New York Times*) criticized this latest entry: "For this Robert Youngson selection of bits and pieces from a score or more comedies made since the mid-1920s by Metro-Goldwyn-Mayer offers some memory-tickling ganders of at least 50 stars… all doing something or other in one or another of their old films.

"But what they do and the sum total of it, while involving the form of comedy, is not unified or very funny, except in occasional spurts. That's because most of the selections are made from sound comedies in which the humor of scenes and situations depends upon an understanding of what has gone before in the way of plot and development of character.

"Mr. Youngson, who has been successful with his previous compilations of silent comedy bits, such as *The Golden Age of Comedy* and *When Comedy Was King*, must know as well as anyone that there is a fundamental difference between the kind of comedy that was played in silent pictures and that that was developed after sound came in. And he must be as aware as any critic that what he has done in this film is no more unified or meaningful than putting together a lot of snatches from old songs."

"Incidentally, the musical score on this picture, prepared by Bernie Green, is cheap and patronizing and the narration, written by Mr. Youngson, is much the same."

Of course, audiences agreed that this was not Youngson's best work, and according to MacGillivray, "Grosses were at a new low, $235,000 in America and another $324,000 worldwide. The film posted a loss of $73,000. The film was composed entirely of old clips – no new, original production at all, except for the titles music, and narration – so it seems incredible that the project could be so costly.

"How could Youngson's big-name *Big Parade* fail with such a goof-proof format? A possible factor might be M-G-M's intensive (and expensive) lab work, preparing and reprinting the dozens of old film scenes. M-G-M maintained its own film-processing unit, so this time the studio (not Youngson) had to pay the lab bills.

"'It was actually *Metro* that lost money on *The Big Parade of Comedy*,' observes John McElwee, 'owing to their own negative cost of $181,000 in the compilation, and the fact that they were splitting revenue with

Youngson. I'd venture *he* came out ahead in the deal, as that $181,000 spent wasn't his, and his deal with M-G-M would have called for him to take a substantial chunk of the rentals. Had *The Big Parade of Comedy* been an in-house project with one of their salaried producers, I think Metro would have come out fine.' "

14

The Fiddle and the Bow

"We'd rather see the original films from which this compilation was collected, but because we don't see too many silents on TV these days, we'll settle for this hash of some of Laurel and Hardy's best bits."

– TV movie listing, *Chicago Tribune*,
July 31, 1984

LAUREL WOULD AGREE, as this newspaper reviewer, that anyone would have preferred the original films to compiled clips. However, it has been reported that he was quite surprised and gratified to see the resurgence of interest in his comedies with Hardy thanks to the Youngson's compilations.

The musical comparison of Laurel & Hardy to a fiddle and a bow originated from a *New York Times* piece, which stated that the pair created comedy symphonies as skinny Laurel the bow played against fat Hardy the fiddle.

A few months after Laurel's death in 1965, Youngson's sixth compilation, *Laurel and Hardy's Laughing 20s*, is released. The film is touted in the advertising as having the most laughs of any comedy, clocked officially at 253.

In a November 3, 1991 revival theater screening, the *Los Angeles Times* calls it, "One of Robert Youngson's best compilation films: vintage silent comedy from the true Golden Age of the nonpareil screen dimwits."

Crowther, *New York Times*, November 18, 1965: "I AM not quite the nut about the old films of Stan Laurel and Oliver Hardy that some people seem to be. A little bit off the dry and bland shenanigans of these two comics goes a long way with me. That's why I am less than limp from laughing after seeing Robert Youngson's latest job of compilation of silent comedies.

"...And too much of it is repetitious. Mr. Youngson has not served them well by taking too many chunks from pictures that are too much alike.

"He has also cut into this compilation several sequences from films of Charlie Chase, one of the lesser known silent comedians, and from films of Max Davidson, a baggy-pants Jewish comedian who looks awfully antique today.

"Since all of the film used is silent, Mr. Youngson has added a sound track that burbles with chatty, cute narration and assails the ears with a tinny musical score. It all but includes instructions telling us when to laugh. There are plenty of places in the stuff with Laurel and Hardy when laughter is likely to be provoked – good, happy barks at neat surprise – but let us spot them ourselves. Don't push."

Back on December 3, 1965, a *New York Times* ad for the film offered reviews:

> 'HAPPINESS IS A THING CALLED LAUREL & HARDY'S LAUGHING 20'S!' – Judith Crist, *Herald Tribune*
>
> 'BEST OF THE TEAM'S COMEDY!' – Francis Herridge, *Post*
>
> 'IT'S GREAT FUN!' – Rose Pelswick, *Journal American*
>
> 'FUNNIEST SHOW IN TOWN' – William Wolf, *Cue Magazine*
>
> '3 ½ Stars! FUN FILLED!' – Kathleen Carroll, *Daily News*
>
> 'NOTHING COULD BE MORE WELCOME!' – Arthur Knight, *Saturday Review*
>
> 'A RIOT!' – William Peper, *World-Telegram*"

On February 14, 1966, a *Los Angeles Times* ad reads: " 'THE LAUGHS ARE NOW – ALL OVER TOWN!' 'FILM 1ST!!!' 'Metro-Goldwyn-Mayer presents a Robert Youngson Production,' 'THE BEST OF STAN & OLLIE,' '253 SOLID LAUGHS ACTUALLY CLOCKED IN SWORN SURVEY!' "

The *Boston Herald* noted the film is, "something to see if you just want to relax and laugh and not worry about a thing."

MacGillivray: "Youngson's Laurel & Hardy feature reached out to the team's international fan base, which responded enthusiastically. *Laughing '20s* became Robert Youngson's biggest success, with domestic business ($431,000 gross) just shy of the *When Comedy Was King* benchmark, but worldwide business ($1,200,000 gross) surpassing it. Youngson spent only $75,000 to make the film, so a profit was assured. 'Again, there were greater costs attendant,' says John McElwee, 'upon considerable showmanship efforts expended on the film's behalf, and although final profits were the highest so far ($361,000), there was still a split [due Youngson, leaving] less for Metro.' "

The compilation received attention again when PBS broadcast the film as a special to attract new subscribers. *New York Times*, March 9, 1984, John J. O'Connor reported: "*Laughing 20s*… is an old M-G-M film with a determinedly bouncy style reminiscent of those venerable *Pete Smith Specialties* that used to be a staple in movie houses. Its observations stay safely on the surface. Watching Laurel and Hardy walk away from the camera, the narrator sees them going off 'into the distance and into memory – we will never see their like again.'

"…Clearly, Stan and Ollie got better as they went along, and this 'biography' is at its best with clips from movies at the end of the 20s, most notably from *Liberty* and its teetering high jinks on the top floor of a skeletal building frame. Whether disappearing into mysteriously deep street puddles or triggering a massive pie-throwing fracas, slow-burning Ollie and goofy Stan remain irresistibly zany creations – even in this uneven survey."

Laurel & Hardy's Laughing 20s does not have any narration over the title credits, but the film does retain Chopin's Étude in C Major, Opus 10, No. 3. However, the familiar Laurel & Hardy theme is interspersed with Chopin in the arrangement. The film opens presenting Laurel & Hardy's separate appearances starting with Hardy's 1915's *Fatty's Fatal Fun*. Hardy joined Roach in mid-1920s. We see excerpts of 1927's *Putting Pants on Philip*. This is the first film where the two were paired by accident.

At the start of the clips of Hardy alone, the narrator begins: "Through a cardboard door out of the past steps a beaming moon-faced 23-year old comedian named Oliver Norville Hardy. Oliver announces he is to be married in this comedy called *Fatty's Fatal Fun*, made two World Wars ago in 1915 when life and the movies were both much simpler.

"Babe Hardy, as he was then known, made a striking figure in his striped pants and cut-away coat, and even a plausible though plump lover. But he was an obscure comedian in those days – one of the unknown hundreds who dashed madly about in the deluge of minor comedies that flooded the silent screen. Fame, stardom and an immortal partnership with Stan Laurel lay some 12 long years and uncountable pratfalls, pins in the pants, and pies in the face ahead. Young Stan Laurel looked like this at the beginning of the decade which silent comedy at its height was to make the laughing 20s...."

Stan and Ollie (both alone and together) have the lion's share of footage in this compilation. The film has clips from many shorts, including *Fatty's Fatal Fun* (1915), *Kill or Cure* (1923), *Along Came Auntie* (1926), *45 Minutes from Hollywood* (1926), *Sugar Daddies* (1927), *Call of the Cuckoo* (1927), *Never the Dames Shall Meet* (1927), *Pass the Gravy* (1927), *Dumb Daddies* (1928), *From Soup to Nuts* (1928), *Habeas Corpus* (1928), *Leave 'em Laughing* (1928), *The Finishing Touch* (1928), *Two Tars* (1928), *Double Whoopee* (1929), *Liberty* (1929), *Snappy Sneezer* (1929), *Wrong Again* (1929), and *Thicker Than Water* (1935).

The scenes in the final part of this compilation are re-used from *The Golden Age of Comedy*; such as from *The Second Hundred Years* (1927), *You're Darn Tootin'* (1927), *Two Tars* (1928), *We Faw Down* (1929), and a re-edit from *Battle of the Century* (1927).

There are also appearances by Chase, Davidson, Edgar Buchanan, Viola Richard, Vivien Oakland, Garvin, Kennedy, Dorothy Coburn, and Kay Deslys.

The ending narration to *Laurel & Hardy's Laughing 20s* is sparse. As the pair run off to escape from their wives, the narrator says rather blandly, "Into the distance, and into memory, we will never see their like again." The final portion of Chopin's Étude in C Major, Opus 10, No. 3 is played poignantly on a banjo, leaving us once again with those nostalgic feelings of longing and sadness. The film ends with Laurel pulling the title card across the screen. It reads: "*Laurel & Hardy's Laughing 20s*, THE END, A Robert Youngson Production."

15

The Return of the Fiddle and the Bow

"...Hardy playing a simpering, overweight maiden or a mustachioed villain, or Laurel as a rough-tough bum, should be an unaccustomed sight for the sore eyes of any fan, callow or hip."

– A. H. Weiler, *New York Times*, April 1, 1968

IN 1967, TWO YEARS AFTER his first full feature devoted to Laurel & Hardy, Youngson returned with his seventh compilation feature, *The Further Perils of Laurel & Hardy*. It continued his focus on the team, this time introducing rare footage of Hardy in 1915 and Laurel in 1918 before they became a comedy team, as well as clips with their combined talents.

The excerpts are from *The Hobo* (1917), *The Villain* (1917), *His Day Out* (1918), *Just Rambling Along* (1918), *Do Detectives Think* (1927), *Sugar Daddies* (1927), *The Second Hundred Years* (1927), *You're Darn Tootin'* (1927), *Early to Bed* (1928), *Flying Elephants* (1928), *Habeas Corpus* (1928), *Leave 'em Laughing* (1928), *Should Married Men Go Home?* (1928), *Angora Love* (1929), and *That's My Wife* (1929).

Although Stan and Ollie are the featured attraction, other comics seen include Pollard in *Full o' Pep* (1922), *Stage Struck* (1922), and *The Anvil Chorus* (1922); Harlow in *The Unkissed Man* (1929), and Chase in *The Way of All Pants* (1927). In addition, there is appearances by Jimmy Aubrey, Finlayson, Edgar Kennedy, Tom Kennedy, Jimmie 'Paul' Parrott, Charlie Rogers, Bryant Washburn, West, and Noah Young.

This time a problem arose for Youngson as Fox's publicity department did not do justice to this compilation. Their marketing department now appealed to the youth audience, so this title had little coverage. The kiddie matinee trade became the focus of the department's plugging.

MacGillivray observed, "Each of Youngson's films had contained a different combination of ingredients, and if the results were variable, at least they were unique. However, when it became apparent that Laurel and Hardy were the main selling point of Youngson's films, the producer forsook his ambitious historical mosaics. His next feature for Fox would be a strictly commercial venture."

In "Stan and Ollie Formed a Cult," *The Washington Post, Times Herald*, December 8, 1967, Richard L. Coe reported, "…you're guaranteed some laughs in this one." However, Coe had issues with the soundtrack and narration.

Coe: "This remains hilarious stuff, both broad and subtle, but watching it I often resented the soundtrack. As was the case with *Laurel and Hardy's Laughing 20s*, this was pieced together by producer-writer Robert Youngson and, since he's clearly done some research, I suppose we'll have to accept his judgment.

"By snipping, however, from *Leave 'em Laughing, Habeas Corpus, That's My Life* and a batch of lesser known items, Youngson could be depriving us of a sense of wholeness for individual two-reelers at the cost of repeating like sequences. I find the music loud and obvious (why all the Gilbert and Sullivan, strictly of previous generations) and the narration superlatives can kill points which the team makes adequately in its brilliant mime."

Weiler's review on April 1, 1968 first noted that "This latest culling of their many silent films may be overshadowed by the fact that their singular clowning in similar capers has not only been a familiar staple on TV's home screens but has also turned up in theaters over the last two years in another couple of full-length collections.:"

Referring to Youngson and his compilations, Weiler complained: "Unfortunately, that imprimatur has become worn from overexposure. And what has been true of previous compilations applies to this one: The muscular slapstick, the pie in the face, the falling into mudholes are funny – but not out of context, not for 99 minutes. And vintage views of the late Jean Harlow, Charlie Chase and Snub Pollard may be mildly mirthful, but they are dragged in simply to indicate the kind of frenetic, off-the-cuff comedy turned out in the Hal Roach Studio during the Laurel and Hardy era.

"...Mr. Youngson's candid and instructive commentary is spoken with proper irreverence by Jay Jackson. John Parker's musical background may be too intrusive on occasion, but it makes an appropriately tinny and jazzy comment on the hectic goings-on. They all prove that, while a good deal of the action is simply hectic, a fair portion of it is still a pleasure."

In "Slapstick That Sticks," Vincent Canby (*New York Times*, October 12, 1969), weighed in. Canby observed, "During the last 10 years or so, movie producers have been ravaging Laurel and Hardy features and shorts for scenes that they have then compiled into anthology features, some more lovingly and intelligently put together (Robert Youngson's *The Golden Age of Comedy* and *The Further Perils of Laurel and Hardy*) than others, especially Jay Ward's *The Crazy World of Laurel and Hardy*... .

"[The latter] (1966) is all peaks and no valleys, bits and pieces from too many comedies, climaxes presented without lead-ins, a kind of surreal symphony of immersions, skull fractures, shattered windows, punctured posteriors and zonk-pow-splat sound effects. Laurel and Hardy seemed as grotesque and brutal now as they seemed when I was a child."

Canby reported that Hal Roach Studios was re-releasing their feature *Way Out West* with five of their shorts. Ultimately, he captures the essence of what is definitely the only legitimate criticism of compilations like Youngson's.

Canby: "The most obvious virtue of the program is that it presents Laurel and Hardy unedited, complete in their own time and space, rather than excised and juxtaposed in ways that destroy the very conscious, internal rhythms of their gags." Canby further offers Charles Barr's point in *Laurel and Hardy* (University of California Press) discussing the team's " 'triple gag,' in which gags are set, one within another, like Chinese boxes...

"Youngson, by using longer excerpts from individual films, made some quite delightful anthologies, but nothing is as satisfactory as seeing the best of the original films, unaltered and unedited, as is this reissued program from Roach."

The Further Perils of Laurel & Hardy does not start as the early compilations, such as the nostalgic-sounding strains of Chopin's familiar Étude in C, Major, Opus 10, No. 3 played over the credits. Instead, it begins with an extended scene from the Laurel & Hardy short *You're Darn Tootin.'* In addition, the narration does not begin for more than five minutes while we have been watching a segment with the Boys playing instruments at a concert.

After Hardy finally retrieves his music sheet from under the conductor's feet, the narrator opens the film: " 'I can't play without it,' explains Oliver. 'My soul is hushed.' So with immortal music ringing in our ears, we begin our cavalcade of classic comedy moments, unseen for forty years. Films so old we think you'll find them fresh and new. Here then are *The Further Perils of Laurel & Hardy.* "

With the credit titles done, a scene from another short is shown. Narrator: "A Max Sennett bathing beauty appears to pose prettily for Charlie Chaplin on a summer afternoon in 1915. Actually, it is a double deception: The beauty is really young Oliver Hardy in his third year as a supporting comedian. The admirer counting the curves is Billy West, who with uncanny accuracy imitated Chaplin's walk, mannerisms, and even his plots. This tale of a country girl's deception resembles *Tillie's Punctured Romance*. Little Miss Gingham bounces into the general store. In comedy's golden days, the best comedians; Chaplin, Keaton, Arbuckle, Langdon, all impersonated woman at one time or another… ."

As an example of the then "new sophistication in comedy" and a brief break from the Boys' films, the narrator notes, "Charlie Chase was the master of the comedy of embarrassment, and at one time, the most popular star of two reelers in the world. Today he is strangely and unfairly forgotten."

Similar to *Laurel & Hardy's Laughing 20s*, *The Further Perils of Laurel & Hardy* has longer segments from their comedies as compared to the earlier compilations. At times, this does seem to weigh down the films and makes viewing them seem a little tedious at times.

With "Auld Lang Syne" played as background accompaniment, the narrator closes the film by saying, "The jovial fat one and his sad skinny partner have long since departed, but the laughter undiminished roars on. On strips of film where time stands still, they have left their shadows behind."

The differences to previous compilations came at the box office as well. MacGillivray: "The financial returns, accordingly, were reduced. In other countries the Laurel & Hardy names brought in a worthy $463,000 gross, but in America the film fetched only a languid $165,000 gross, thanks to Fox's limited release.

"Robert Youngson had been issuing new features about every 18 months. After the indifferent release of *Further Perils*, Youngson took more time off before tackling his next project."

Although he was still critical, Everson offered some pages devoted to Youngson's films in his Laurel & Hardy book published at the time of Youngson's all-out mining of the team's footage. Everson now seemed reluctant to accept the Youngson method influenced by newsreels, although by now Youngson seemed to make the narration less obvious and over-written.

Everson: "One can quibble with some of Youngson's methods: the earlier films tended to be overburdened with unnecessary (albeit informative and seriously intended) narration, and too often carefully built and methodically developed comedy sequences were edited to the bone, rushing right to the crux of the jokes, as though Laurel & Hardy were all speed, violence, and fast slapstick.

"But a compilation is a film apart, with a responsibility to itself as well as to its source material; it must create its own pattern and rhythm, and too much time devoted to an individual ingredient means both a disruption of that rhythm, and a less generous totality of highlights. Laurel & Hardy purists may well dispute Youngson's handling of certain favorite and well-remembered sequences, but there can be no disputing the taste and love he has put into these compilations, the skill with which they have been edited, or the unbounded delight they have brought to audiences who have been introduced to Laurel & Hardy for the first time through them."

16

The End of the Rope

"I have a feeling, way down deep, that he had come to the end of his rope, creative-wise. After the last one [*4 Clowns*], he kind of *talked* doing a movie, but he never did anything concrete about going ahead and doing it. And I wonder if maybe he didn't think that it had been done at that point. Maybe he couldn't have gone any further."

– Jeanne Keyes Youngson told Scott MacGillivray

IN 1970, *4 CLOWNS*, Youngson's last compilation, honored a quartet of film funnymen. Of course, Laurel & Hardy are two of them. The others are Charlie Chase and Buster Keaton.

The excerpts included Hardy in *The Hobo* (1917), *His Day Out* (1918) and *No Man's Law* (1927); Laurel in *Kill or Cure* (1923); Laurel & Hardy in *Putting Pants on Philip* (1927), *The Second Hundred Years* (1927), *Their Purple Moments* (1928), *Two Tars* (1928), *Big Business* (1929), and *Double Whoopie* (1929).

Chase is seen in *What Price Goofy* (1925), *Fluttering Hearts* (1927, with Hardy), *One Mama Man* (1927), *Us* (1927), *The Family Group* (1928), *Limousine Love* (1928) and *Movie Night* (1929); and an extended sequence from Keaton's *Seven Chances* (1925) ends the compilation.

Others seen in the clips are Chaplin imitator West in *His Day Out* (1918) and *The Hobo* (1917); Rex the Wonder Horse in *No Man's Land* (1927), Dent, Leatrice Joy, Barbara Kent, Don Likes, Viola Richard, and Tiny Sandford.

Youngson finally used some footage from Chase's *Limousine Love*. He tried to use the 1928 film as far back as his first compilation. The preview audiences did not care for it, so it was edited out.

The use of the Keaton's *Seven Chances* meant he had to buy the rights from Rohauer, and give him the credit of Associate Producer. As a result, Youngson had to reduce costs elsewhere because of the high cost to get to use this footage. Even worse concerning the acquisition it is that Rohauer did not even allow Fox to own the film outright, but merely licensed it to Fox for twenty years and thus the film now has been withdrawn from distribution.

Everson told MacGillivray: "He never commented about that. I don't say this critically, but he felt that everything he did was tremendous, and if he had to cut down on production values, he was adding enough in terms of new material to make up for it. I don't think he really felt that he was shortchanging the public, or cutting down in an obvious way."

As with his previous compilation, this final one did not get the right promotion. Once again, Fox senselessly offered the film to the kiddie market in its publicity campaign. MacGillivray: "Fox didn't place any ads for *4 Clowns* at all, making only a token effort to sell the film. Exhibitors were given a skimpy pressbook and very little showmanship. The coming-attractions trailer was narrated not by the mature Jay Jackson but by a younger, more lightweight announcer."

4 Clowns opens with films of real life on the streets. Narrator: "In 1900, when these films were made on New York's Fifth Avenue, two newly-born inventions were just beginning to shape and expand our lives: the automobile and the motion picture.

"We're traveling up turn-of-the-century Broadway, a street already world-famous for its swank restaurants, legitimate theatres, and electric lights. The first movie houses were not to be found here, but on the side streets. The lowly nickelodeon catered to the common man and from the beginning comedy was king.

"Films had to be hand-cranked by a projectionist. In this early French comedy, someone steals into the Paris conservatory to make the great master clock run fast, which speeds up time everywhere in the city."

The credits roll over speeded-up film scenes to the musical accompaniment of Jacques Offenbach's "Infernal Galop" (from "Orpheus in the Underworld"), best known as the tune associated with the French Can-Can.

After the credits, the narrator returns, saying, "What a difference two decades made. This is Fifth Avenue in the 1920s. The automobile had driven the horse from the streets to the racetrack. And this is Broadway in evolution through the roaring 20s as it might have been viewed if we're riding H.G. Wells' time machine... ."

For the film's conclusion, the narrator disappointingly does not generalize about the era as in the early compilations. To the final scene from Keaton's *Seven Chances* ending, the narrator merely explains the film's outcome. Narrator: "Married in the nick of time; eternal happiness, love, wealth, no worries, except keeping out of the way of a few thousand disgruntled brides." The end title card appears. Unlike the first compilations, and like the last few films, Youngson disbanded with his characteristic nostalgic narration. Clearly, this production, and the last few compilations, suffered from this bland conclusion.

MacGillivray concluded, "Although Youngson economized on the production, he had probably assured a personal profit in advance by offering the film to Fox as part of a two-picture deal (*Further Perils*, then *4 Clowns*) and negotiating a price up front, leaving Fox to sell the films later at their own rates. Fox finally released *4 Clowns* in September 1970. It's a good thing Youngson didn't depend on a percentage of rental revenues from *4 Clowns*, because the returns were pitiful. Fox probably didn't make the film available to many international theaters, and took in only $155,000 in grosses from the *entire* world market outside America. The less said about the American run, the better: *4 Clowns* brought in a heartbreaking $74,000 – *before* expenses – clearly signaling the end of the line.

"'The fact that Youngson was able to find distribution for his projects over a 13-year period is a testament to his ability and the appeal of his compilations,' John McElwee concludes, 'but they never would have been considered major projects by companies that handled them, and revenue expectation – along with profits realized – would have borne out that truth.'

After *4 Clowns*, another film had been a possibility using the M-G-M silent material. MacGillivray notes: "He approached M-G-M with a proposal for a feature-length cavalcade of thrills, a dramatic companion piece to *M-G-M's Big Parade of Comedy*." The working title: *There's Nothing Like The Movies*."

Everson told MacGillivray: "When he had access to all the Metro material he obviously saw a chance to do something really worthwhile, because at that time none of those M-G-M silents had ever appeared on television. In the interim, the Chaneys and the Garbos and certain others have become fairly regular on television, tape and laser disc, but at the time it was completely novel."

Sometime in 1974, reportedly the ten-reel workprint film without a soundtrack apparently was shelved as his health declined.

Robert Youngson's fascinating output of compilations had come to an end and perhaps sooner than one might expect.

17

Afterword

SINCE HIS DEATH nearly forty-five years ago in 1974, Robert Youngson has been paid little attention. He is a forgotten soul as far as the print world is concerned. That is true, with the exception of the chapter devoted to him in MacGillivray's superb Laurel & Hardy book, and an excellent scholarly piece by Brent Walker offering a short biography and focusing on identifying the excerpts used in the compilations.

Perhaps the only known time after his death in which Youngson's shorts would receive airtime is on February 4, 1979 (9 p.m.) in a new series called *Academy Leaders*. The latter showcased Academy Award-winning and nominated shorts debuted on PBS with host Norman Corwin.

One of the shorts played was Youngson's 1948 one-reeler *Spills and Chills*, which focused on stunts and daredevil turns. Gary Arnold (in "Short and Sweet") noted: "*Spills and Chills* has been recycled frequently but it's still a lively survey. Repetition cannot stale certain death-defying feats, like Lilian Boyer's insouciant performances on a rope ladder dangling from the wing of a biplane."

Charles Champlin, *Los Angeles Times*, February 5, 1979 said, "*Spills and Chills* is comedy relief… of stunt-flying, wing-walking, high-diving and other forms of brave and stomach-grabbing madness, as watched by newsreel photographers."

More importantly, Champlin explained: "By an irony we could do without, the short film is a versatile, powerful, likable, invaluable and endangered form. It can produce all the same emotions from hilarity (particularly) to sorrow that the long form evokes, and it can handle themes and stories that would be diluted or commercially unworkable at feature length.

"But the rise of the double-feature, and after that the need to turn over the audiences fast at single features, did in the theatrical short subject."

Although Youngson's prime skill in writing and producing the short subject has lost its theatrical venue seemingly now forever, the feature-length film remains. Perhaps, some day in a neighborhood theater near you, a revival of silent film comedy will return. When it does, the one unsung hero to remember is the man that made it first a reality. The man who gave us perhaps the greatest compilations ever made will receive his due.

Though Youngson and the 1920s world that he never tired of remembering have vanished completely, his films celebrating that time remain with us and are as vibrant and enjoyable now more than ever.

When you get a chance some evening, please pay Youngson and the world of the 1920s comedy greats a private tribute. You can do that by treating yourself kindly by screening one of his remarkably enjoyable compilations with a few big soft pretzels. If you do, you will be acknowledging a fine talented filmmaker who indulged himself (perhaps too much so) with food, film and a bygone world of his childhood. Unfortunately, he quickly resembled the overweight comics, like Hardy, that he so admired and kept alive in his compilations.

Although he left us before any real appreciation would come about, at least the producer-writer left us a treasure chest of pleasure in his unforgettable productions. I hope that the peak of his life's work, the silent film comedy compilations, which are so full of love and laughter, may touch your life as it has mine.

Robert Youngson aptly ended his personal favorite, *When Comedy Was King*, with the narrator saying, "So ends our visit to the era of the great silent clowns who mass produced laughter and sold happiness, and who passed into oblivion just before the years when the world needed them most."

Undoubtedly, this is true today, more than ever. Thank you, Mr. Robert Youngson, for superbly celebrating that vanished world!

Appendices

Selected Bibliography

William K. Everson, *The Films of Laurel and Hardy* (Citadel Press, 1967).

Joe Franklin, *Classics of the Silent Screen* (Citadel Press, 1959).

Scott MacGillivray, *Laurel & Hardy: From the Forties Forward, Second Edition, Revised and Expanded*, (iUniverse 2009).

Ronald S. Magliozzi and Charles L. Turner, "Witnessing the Development of Independent Film Culture in New York: An Interview with Charles L. Turner," *Film History*, Vol. 12, No.1. Oral History (2000), pp. 72-96. (Published by Indiana University Press.)

Leonard Maltin, "*FFM* Interviews Robert Youngson," *Film Fan Monthly*, 1971.

Brent Walker, "The Robert Youngson Compilations: Identification of Film Sources, *The Moving Image: The Journal of the Association of Moving Image Archivists*, Vol. 2, No. 1 (Spring 2002), pp. 130-174. (Published by University of Minnesota Press.)

Cameo and Puzzums

TWO OF THE MOST UNUSUAL comedy moments in Youngson's compilations come from the non-human actors. Here is some additional information on two of these endearing performers.

CAMEO, THE WONDER DOG (1919 – 2/18/1935)

Brent Walker said, "Cameo may have been the greatest dog comedian ever to work in films (one contemporary article called Cameo 'The Buster Keaton of Dogdom'... Cameo was a highly gifted dog whose ability to perform comedic gags far surpassed any canine actors before or since."
    Even though Cameo was referred to in films as "he," the dog was a female Boston bull terrier. His real name was Camisole owned and trained by Hap Ward.

SELECTED FILMOGRAPHY:

Heroes of the Street (1922)
Nip and Tuck (1923) – short, scene used in *The Golden Age of Comedy* (poker game and money chase), he was 3 ½ years old when she made this film.
Asleep at the Switch (1923) – short, uncredited, scene in *Days of Thrills and Laughter* (smoking cigar and then playing checkers)
Smile Please (1924) – uncredited

The Hollywood Kid (1924) – short, billed as Cameo the Wonder Dog
The Lion and the Souse (1924) – short
Broadway Beauties (1924) – short
A Self-Made Failure (1924) (w/Lloyd Hamilton)
Conductor 1492 (1924) (w/Johnny Hines)
Smile (1924)
How Baxter Butted In (1925)
Little Annie Rooney (1925) (w/Mary Pickford)
Frisco Sally Levy (1927)
Penrod and Sam (1931) playing Penrod's dog Duke
Misbehaving Ladies (1931)

PUZZUMS (THE CAT) (1926 - 1934)

Puzzums was a grey cat, and she became Mack Sennett Studios cat in the late 1920s, replacing Pepper. The owner was Miss Nadine Dennis. Her life was cut short as she reportedly died from an infected tooth.

SELECTED FILMOGRAPHY:

The Girl from Everywhere (1927)
Love at First Flight (1928) (landed a plane)
The Girl from Nowhere (1928)
His Unlucky Night (1928) Scene used in *The Golden Age of Comedy* (played checkers w/Andy Clyde)
The Chicken (1928)
The Bargain Hunt (1928)
The Campus Vamp (1928)
Calling Hubby's Bluff (1929)
The Dog Doctor (1929)
Handy Andy (1934) (w/Will Rogers)

An interesting article on Puzzums is reprinted here. It was first published in *The New Movie Magazine*, July 1932, page 12):

Two Cats of Hollywood

By Joan Tracy

"**Not rival film beauties** but two regular felines who found fame and fortunes in Hollywood and brought stardom by proxy to their mistress."

"This is the story of the two most famous cats in Hollywood – and of their mistress, to whom they brought stardom by proxy.... .

When Nadine Dennis was a little girl, she dreamed of the day when she would go to Hollywood and become a motion picture actress. A leading lady – and even, perhaps a star!

It was not new – the dream. All over the world, in cities, in the country, in towns both large and small, other girls were living and dreaming the same sort of youthful, schoolgirl dreams... .

Hollywood was not big enough for all of them. Its starry firmament could not hold so many luminaries... . Nadine Dennis became just another one of the eager, striving girls who were putting their youth and their glorious fresh beauty against the cold cruelty of the cameras – pitting their all and losing.

And Nadine Dennis might have been just like most of those others – lost and forgotten in the struggle. But because of a gentle, kindly deed, performed several years ago, she remains in Hollywood today, comfortably, happily, and with an income that is far from negligible... .

In 1926, during the cold grey hours of an October dawn, Nadine Dennis was awakened by wails and moans that came from somewhere in the fields near her window. At first she thought it was a trapped rat, but when she investigated she found a newly born kitten, half frozen from the cold, almost dead from starvation.

Picking up the poor, pitiful little animal, she carried it to her home and gave it into the keeping of her highly-prized Persian cat, which only a few days before had kittens of her own.

Of high pedigree and royal lineage, the Persian frowned upon the mongrel kitten, and refused to allow it among her brood. But Nadine cared for it tenderly, feeding it from a bottle, until it was old enough to lap up milk by itself.

One of the Persian's kittens, Ko-Fan, began to play with the little waif, which Nadine had named Puzzums, and the two cats became inseparable.

In fact, Nadine could not leave them even to go to the studios in her daily search for work.

Occasionally, her efforts were rewarded, and she obtained an obscure bit in some production. And while she was performing before the cameras, the two cats would sit in the sidelines, waiting quietly for her to finish.

And then one day, an assistant director noticed them, and suggested that she show them to Mack Sennett, who could use them in his comedies.

At first she did not give the suggestion much consideration. After all, she was in Hollywood to get in pictures herself, not to train cats for movies. But the more she thought of it, the more she was inclined to give the idea a trial.

Acting on a hunch one day, she made the long trip out to the Sennett studio, where she was immediately offered a contract for Puzzums at the stupendous salary of $50 for the first week, graduating to $250 a week by the end of three years, the term of the agreement.

Today, Nadine Dennis has given up all intention of striving for stardom for herself. She has a comfortable home – a nice car – pretty clothes and pleasant friends. Her life is very full. She has no financial worries.

And her days are occupied in managing the business affairs of two of the most beautiful stars in Hollywood – The two cats!"

> The article's picture was captioned "Miss Nadine Dennis with Puzzums, the kitten that repaid a debt."
> Also there is a picture with the caption: "Puzzums and Ko-Fan, mongrel and aristocrat, well received in the cinema capital."

Awards

As his alma mater, Youngson was a prize-winning member of the Harvard Film Society.

He also received the Page One Award in Movies, given to him by the Newspaper Guild of New York.

He received two Academy Awards for the short subjects, *The World of Kids* and *This Mechanical Age*.

Credits

FEATURE FILMS

Fifty Years Before Your Eyes (1950) D: Robert G. Youngson.

Narrated by Quentin Reynolds, H.V. Kaltenborn, Dwight Weist, Milton Cross, Norman Brokenshire, Andre Baruch, Clem McCarthy, Dan Donaldson, Arthur Godfrey.

The years 1900 to 1950 are highlighted via selected newsreels. Included is footage of Queen Victoria's funeral and New York City Mayor Fiorella LaGuardia reading the Sunday newspaper comics over the radio. Clips from movies tell America's story from the Pilgrims through the taming of the frontier. A forecast is made of possible World War 3 with the Soviet Union. Additional footage of Enrico Caruso, Charles Chaplin (from a 1915 comedy short, *His New Job*), William F. 'Buffalo Bill' Cody, Calvin Coolidge, Eugene V. Debs, Gertrude Ederle, Dwight D. Eisenhower, Mahatma Gandhi, Thomas Masaryk, Lou Gehrig, Harold 'Red' Grange, Warren G. Harding, Emperor Hirohito, Herbert Hoover, Al Jolson, Kaiser Wilhelm II, V.I. Lenin, Charles A. Lindbergh, Huey Long, William McKinley, Prince Charles, Knute Rockne, Will Rogers, Franklin D. Roosevelt, Theodore Roosevelt, Lillian Russell, Babe Ruth, George Bernard Shaw, Joseph Stalin, Harry S Truman, Czar Nicholas II, Ben Turpin, Rudolph Valentino, Pancho Villa, Helen Wills, Woodrow Wilson.

Screenplay by Alfred Butterfield and Thomas H. Wolf, from a story by Butterfield. Produced by Alfred Butterfield.

Music by Howard Jackson, William Lava.

Released on June 27.
(72 minutes/RCA Sound)
Warner Brothers

"*A connoisseur's collection of the crème de la comedie!*"

The Golden Age of Comedy (1958) D: Robert Youngson.

Narrated by Dwight Weist, Ward Wilson.
An array of silent film players are featured in this parade of clips:

- Billy Bevan in *Super-Hooper-Dyne Lizzies* (1925); *Circus Today* (1926); *Nip and Tuck* (1923).
- Harry Langdon in *Remember When?* (1925); *Luck o' the Foolish* (1924).
- Stan Laurel and Oliver Hardy in *Angora Love* (1929); *Habeas Corpus* (1928); *The Second Hundred Years* (1927); *Double Whoopee* (1929); *We Faw Down* (1928); *You're Darn Tootin'* (1927); *Two Tars* (1928); *Battle of the Century* (1927).
- Will Rogers in *Going to Congress* (1924); *Uncensored Movies* (1923); *Big Moments from Little Pictures* (1924).
- Charley Chase in *The Sting of Stings* (1927).
- Andy Clyde in *His Unlucky Night* (1928).
- Carole Lombard in *Run, Girl, Run* (1928).
- Ben Turpin in *The Jolly Jilter* (1927); *A Harem Knight* (1926); *Yukon Jake* (1924); *Ten Dollars or Ten Days* (1924); *The Prodigal Bridegroom* (1926); *The Daredevil* (1923).

Also seen are Alice Day, Kewpie Morgan, Harry Gribbon, Cameo the Wonder Dog, Puzzums the Cat, Daphne Pollard, Jean Harlow, Jack Richardson, Thelma Hill.
Screenplay by Robert Youngson, who also produced.
Music by George Steiner.
Released on January 8.
(79 minutes/video/laserdisc/DVD)
Distributors Corporation of America

"New York opening smashes 45 year record!"

When Comedy Was King (1960) D: Robert Youngson.

Narrated by Dwight Weist.
　Another package of clips from silent film days, focusing on slapstick comedians.

- Charley Chase in *Movie Night* (1929).
- Charles Chaplin in *The Masquerader* (1914); *His Trysting Place* (1914); *Gentlemen of Nerve* (1914).
- Fatty Arbuckle in *Fatty and Mabel Adrift* (1916).
- Gloria Swanson and Wallace Beery in *Teddy at the Throttle* (1917).
- Harry Langdon in *The First 100 Years* (1924).
- Snub Pollard in *It's a Gift* (1923).
- Edgar Kennedy in *A Pair of Tights* (1929).
- Buster Keaton in *Cops* (1922).
- Ben Turpin in *Yukon Jake* (1924).
- Billy Bevan in *Wall Street Blues* (1924); *Super-Hooper-Dyne Lizzies* (1925); *The Lion's Whiskers* (1925); *Wandering Willies* (1926).
- Stan Laurel and Oliver Hardy in *Big Business* (1929).

Also seen is Mabel Normand, Mack Swain, Chester Conklin, Al [Fuzzy] St. John, Bobby Vernon, Teddy (a dog), Alice Day, Anita Garvin, Stu Erwin, Marion Byron, Vernon Dent, Andy Clyde, Ruth Hiatt, Kewpie Morgan, James Finlayson.
　Screenplay by Robert Youngson, who also produced.
　Music by Ted Royal.
　Released on February 29.
　(81 minutes/video/laserdisc/DVD)
　Robert Youngson Productions/20th Century-Fox

Days of Thrills and Laughter (1961) D: Robert Youngson.

Narrated by Jay Jackson.
　This tribute to Hollywood's silent movies features classic action and comedy scenes. Aside from the clips of individual stars, there is a French silent, *The Bath Chair Man* (1904), which features a city chase involving

three people plus a man taking a bath in a rolling chair. Another clip shows bathing beauties of 1916 playing on the beach and in an indoor pool. Also, additional selections from cliffhanger serials.

- Snub Pollard in *The Movies* (1922); *Spot Cash* (1921); *Blow 'em Up* (1922); *The Joy Riders* (1921); *Late Lodgers* (1921).
- Mabel Normand in *Mabel's Dramatic Career* (1913).
- The Keystone Cops in *Her Torpedoed Love* (1917).
- Charles Chaplin in *The Adventurer* (1917); *The Cure* (1916).
- Douglas Fairbanks Sr. in *Wild and Woolly* (1917).
- Billy Bevan in *Whispering Whiskers* (1926).
- Ben Turpin in *Home Made Movies* (1922); *Asleep at the Switch* (1923).
- Oliver Hardy in *The Hobo* (1917), *Say It with Babies* (1926).
- Stan Laurel in *Kill or Cure* (1923).
- Harry Langdon in *All Night Long* (1924).
- Arthur Stone in *Sherlock Sleuth* (1925).
- Harry Houdini in *The Master Mystery* (1919); *The Man from Beyond* (1922).
- Pearl White in *The Lightning Raider* (1919); *The Perils of Pauline* (1914).
- Ruth Roland in *The Tiger's Tail* (1919); *The Timber Queen* (1922).
- Walter Miller and Boris Karloff in *King of the Kongo* (1929).
- Gladys McConnell in *The Fire Detective* (1929).
- Allene Ray in *The Man Without a Face* (1928); *The Yellow Cameo* (1928).
- Ralph Kellard in *The Shielding Shadow* (1916).
- Monty Banks in *Play Safe* (1927).
- Charley Chase in *Accidental Accidents* (1924).

Also seen are Mack Sennett, Marie Mosquini, Ford Sterling, Dixie Chene, Virginia Fox, Andy Clyde, Noah Young, Al [Fuzzy] St. John, Billy West, Cameo the Wonder Dog, Eddie Lyons, Lee Moran, Billie Rhodes, Al Christie, Crane Wilbur, Bud Jamison, Leo Willis.

Screenplay by Robert Youngson, who also produced.
Music by Jack Shaindlin.
Released on March 21.
(93 minutes/video/DVD)
Robert Youngson Productions/20th Century-Fox

"All together in the film that brings back the belly laugh!"

30 Years of Fun (1963) D: Robert Youngson.

Narrated by Jay Jackson. Vocalist: Bernie Knee [Bernard Green].

Included in this compilation are films from France and Stan Laurel's first pairing with Oliver Hardy in *Lucky Dog* (1921) and Hardy alone in *Why Girls Say No* (1927). We see a steam train on elevated tracks in New York City and an Easter Parade, employees leaving the French film factory of the Lumière Brothers; French soldiers in an army camp; Theodore Roosevelt as a soldier with the Rough Riders and giving a speech to women seeking the vote; the Wright Brothers in one of their airplanes; footage of various French films circa 1904 - 1906; views of San Francisco before and after the earthquake of 1906; early automobiles; the end of World War One; Prohibition; behind the scenes in Hollywood; 1920s dance marathons; and a series of chases.

- Song: "Bring Back the Laughter" (Robert Youngson).
- Charles Chaplin in *The Rink* (1916); *The Floorwalker* (1916); *The Pawnshop* (1916); and *Easy Street* (1917).
- Snub Pollard in *The Jail Bird* (1921) and *Own Your Home* (1921).
- Irving Bacon in *Hurry Doctor* (1925) and *Whispering Whiskers* (1924).
- Harry Langdon in *Feet of Mud* (1924) and *Smile Please* (1924).
- Billy Bevan in *Whispering Whiskers* (1924); *Skinners in Silk* (1925); *One Cylinder Love* (1923); *The Golf Nut* (1927); and *The Best Man* (1928).
- Charley Chase in *Publicity Pays* (1924); *Big Red Riding Hood* (1925); and *Bromo and Juliet* (1926).
- Syd Chaplin in *A Submarine Pirate* (1915).
- Douglas Fairbanks [Sr.] and Mary Pickford in footage from a World War One Liberty Bond campaign.
- Buster Keaton in *The Balloonatic* (1923) and *Daydreams* (1922).
- Carter DeHaven and Flora Parker DeHaven in *Christmas* (1922).
- A star-studded premiere at Grauman's Chinese Theater featuring Jack Holt, Conrad Nagel, Tom Mix, Irving Willat, Billie Dove, Lew Cody, Mabel Normand, King Vidor, Eleanor Boardman, Norma Shearer, Irving Thalberg, Greta Garbo, and John Gilbert.

Also seen are Noah Young, Ralph Graves, Andy Clyde, Harry Gribbon, Lillian Russell, Eric Campbell, President Woodrow Wilson, James Cruze, Wallace Reid, Phyllis Haver, Lloyd Hamilton, Lupino Lane, Thelma Hill, Marie Mosquini, Jackie Lucas, Billy Armstrong, Louise Carver, Texas Guinan, Kewpie Morgan, Marjorie Daw, Creighton Hale, and Max Davidson. Written and produced by Robert Youngson.
Music by Bernard Green, Jack Shaindlin.
Released on February 10.
(85 minutes)
Robert Youngson Productions/20th Century-Fox

MGM's Big Parade of Comedy (1964) D: Robert Youngson.

Narrated by Les Tremayne.

Comedies from the film studio Metro-Goldwyn-Mayer are in the spotlight. Highlights include various vintage scenes re-edited for the studio's 1930s short subjects, including *Goofy Movies* and *Pete Smith Specialties*; and shots of the various movie studios.

- Songs:
"Jean, Oh Jean" (Bernard Green; Robert Youngson).
"Marie" (Green; Youngson).
"Big Parade of Comedy March" (Green; Youngson).
- Larry Semon in *Kid Speed* (1924) and *The Cloudhopper* (1925).
- John Gilbert in *Show People* (1928).
- Joan Crawford in an MGM promotional film and *The Boob* (1926).
- Marion Davies in *The Red Mill* (1927) and *Show People* (1928).
- Karl Dane, George K. Arthur, and Polly Moran in *China Bound* (1929).
- George K. Arthur and Marceline Day in *Detectives* (1928).
- Buster Keaton in *The Cameraman* (1928).
- Charles Chaplin in *Show People* (1928).
- Jimmy Durante in *Hollywood Party* (1934).
- Marie Dressler in *Reducing* (1931) and *Tugboat Annie* (1933).
- Jean Harlow in *Hold Your Man* (1933); *Bombshell* (1933); *Girl from Missouri* (1934); *Suzy* (1936); *Personal Property* (1937); *Libeled Lady* (1936); and *Dinner at Eight* (1933).
- Carole Lombard in *The Gay Bride* (1934).
- The Three Stooges in *Hollywood Party* (1934).

- W.C. Fields in *David Copperfield* (1935).
- Stan Laurel and Oliver Hardy in *Bonnie Scotland* (1935) and *Hollywood Party* (1934).
- Clark Gable in *Too Hot to Handle* (1938).
- Katharine Hepburn and Cary Grant in *The Philadelphia Story* (1940).
- Robert Benchley in *That Inferior Feeling* (1940); *How to Read* (1938); and *A Night at the Movies* (1937).
- A look at the *Thin Man* movies with William Powell, Myrna Loy, and Asta (a dog).
- William Powell and Gail Patrick in *Love Crazy* (1941).
- Bud Abbott and Lou Costello in *Rio Rita* (1942).
- Lucille Ball in *Meet the People* (1944).
- Red Skelton in *A Southern Yankee* (1948).
- Greta Garbo in *Ninotchka* (1939) and *Two-Faced Woman* (1941).
- The Marx Brothers in *Go West* (1940).
- Dave O'Brien in a parade of *Pete Smith Specialties* clips.

Also seen are Bea Lillie, Gus Leonard, Louise Fazenda, Spencer Bell, Lew Cody, Josephine Crowell, Tod Browning, William Haines, Wallace Beery, Franchot Tone, Lionel Barrymore, Robert Taylor, Spencer Tracy, Chester Morris, Melvyn Douglas, Maxine Gates, Snub Pollard. Written by Robert Youngson, who also produced and designed the titles and effects.
Music by Bernard Green.
Released on September 3.
(90 minutes/video)
Metro-*Goldwyn*-Mayer

"You'll laugh your pants off!"

Laurel and Hardy's Laughing 20s (1965) D: Robert Youngson.

Narrated by Jay Jackson.
The immortal Stan and Ollie (both alone and together) have the lion's share of footage in this compilation; including, *Thicker Than Water* (1935); *Fatty's Fatal Fun* (1915); *Kill or Cure* (1923); *Along Came Auntie* (1926); *45 Minutes from Hollywood* (1926); *Sugar Daddies* (1927); *Putting Pants on Philip* (1927); *From Soup to Nuts* (1928); *Call of the Cuckoo* (1927); *Never the Dames Shall Meet* (1927); *Pass the Gravy* (1927); *Wrong Again* (1929);

Snappy Sneezer (1929); *The Finishing Touch* (1928); *Liberty* (1929); *Dumb Daddies* (1928); *Double Whoopee* (1929); *Leave 'em Laughing* (1928); *Two Tars* (1928); *Habeas Corpus* (1928); *The Second Hundred Years* (1927); *You're Darn Tootin'* (1928); *Battle of the Century* (1927); and *We Faw Down* (1929).

Also seen are Glenn Tryon, Vivien Oakland, Charley Chase, Viola Richard, Anita Garvin, Max Davidson, Edgar Kennedy, Dorothy Coburn, Kay Deslys. Written and produced by Robert Youngson.

Music by Skeets Alquist.
Released in June.
(90 minutes/video/DVD)
Robert Youngson Productions/Metro-*Goldwyn*-Mayer

The Further Perils of Laurel and Hardy (1967)
D: (Robert Youngson).

Narrated by Jay Jackson.
Stan and Ollie are the featured attraction once again. There is also footage of other movie personalities of the era.

- Stan Laurel and Oliver Hardy (alone and together): *Habeas Corpus* (1928); *You're Darn Tootin'* (1927); *The Villain* (1917); *The Hobo* (1917); *His Day Out* (1918); *Just Rambling Along* (1918); *Flying Elephants* (1928); *Sugar Daddies* (1927); *Do Detectives Think* (1927); *The Second Hundred Years* (1927); *Leave 'em Laughing* (1928); *That's My Wife* (1929); *Angora Love* (1929); *Should Married Men Go Home?* (1928); and *Early to Bed* (1928).
- Snub Pollard in *The Anvil Chorus* (1922); *Stage Struck* (1922); and *Full o' Pep* (1922).
- Jean Harlow in *The Unkissed Man* (1929).
- Charley Chase in *The Way of All Pants* (1927).

Also seen are Charlie Rogers, Billy West, Jimmie 'Paul' Parrott, Tom Kennedy, Noah Young, James Finlayson, Bryant Washburn, Jimmy Aubrey, Edgar Kennedy. Written and produced by Robert Youngson.

Music by John [Carl] Parker.
Released in October.
(99 minutes)
Robert Youngson Productions/20th Century-Fox

"These are the 4 clowns who made the Roaring '20s roar!"

4 Clowns (1970) D: Robert Youngson.

Narrated by Jay Jackson.
A quartet of film funnymen are honored in this film: Stan Laurel, Oliver Hardy, Charley Chase, and Buster Keaton.

- Oliver Hardy in *His Day Out* (1918); *The Hobo* (1917); and *No Man's Law* (1927).
- Stan Laurel in *Kill or Cure* (1923).
- Laurel and Hardy in *The Second Hundred Years* (1927); *Big Business* (1929); *Double Whoopie* (1929); *Putting Pants on Philip* (1927); *Two Tars* (1928); and *Their Purple Moments* (1928).
- Charley Chase in *Us* (1927); *One Mama Man* (1927); *What Price Goofy* (1925); *Fluttering Hearts* (1927, with Oliver Hardy); *Movie Night* (1929); *The Family Group* (1928); and *Limousine Love* (1928).
- Buster Keaton in *Seven Chances* (1925).

Also seen are Billy West, Leatrice Joy, Don Likes, Barbara Kent, Rex (King of the Wild Horses), Tiny Sandford, Vernon Dent. Written and produced by Robert Youngson.
Music by Manny Albam.
Released in September.
(97 minutes/Rated [G])
Robert Youngson Productions/20th Century-Fox

SHORT SUBJECTS

Football Magic (1948) D: Robert Youngson.
Narrated by Dan Donaldson.
A documentary look at some gridiron action from high school, college, and professional games. Produced by Walton C. Ament.
Released on September 14.
(20 minutes)
Warner Brothers

Roaring Wheels (1948) D: Robert Youngson.
Narrated by Jackson Beck.
A parade of past champions of the car-racing world. Produced by Walton C. Ament.
Released on October 2.
(10 minutes)
Warner Brothers

Ski Devils (1948) D: Robert Youngson.
Narrated by Dan Donaldson.
This documentary featurette takes to the snow with footage of skiing sportsmen. Produced by Walton C. Ament.
Released on December 4.
(10 minutes)
Warner Brothers

Swim Parade (1949) D: Robert Youngson.
Narrated by Dan Donaldson.
Top performers in swimming and diving are featured, as well as their swimwear styles, Produced by Walton C. Ament.
Released on February 5.
(10 minutes)
Warner Brothers

Batter Up (1949) D: Robert Youngson.
Narrated by Dan Donaldson.
The past year in baseball is highlighted by a series of impressive plays leading up to the 1948 World Series. Written by Robert Youngson. Entry in the *Sports News Reviews* series.
Released on April 9.
(10 minutes)
Vitaphone/Warner Brothers

They're Off (1949) D: Robert Youngson.
Narrated by Dan Donaldson and Clem McCarthy.
The greatest horse races in the sport of kings are featured. Produced by Walton C. Ament.
Released on June 8.
(10 minutes)

Warner Brothers

Spills and Chills (1949) D: Robert Youngson.
Narrated by Dan Donaldson.
    A parade of sports thrills, which include stunt flying and other dangerous endeavors, are featured. Written by Robert Youngson. Produced by Walton C. Ament. Entry in the *Sports News Reviews* series.
    Academy Award Nomination: (Short Subject—One Reel) Walton C. Ament.
    Released on August 13.
    (10 minutes/DVD)
    Warner Brothers

Pigskin Passes (1949) D: Robert Youngson.
Narrated by Dan Donaldson.
    Outstanding football players and games from the past are featured. Produced by Walton C. Ament.
    Released on September 24.
    (18 minutes)
    Warner Brothers

A-Speed on the Deep (1949) D: Robert Youngson.
Narrated by Dwight Weist.
    Fun in the water, including skiing and sailing.
    Released on December 24.
    (10 minutes)
    Warner Brothers

Shoot the Basket! (1950) D: Robert Youngson.
Basketball falls under the spotlight, including professional, high school, and college games. Produced by Walton C. Ament. Entry in the *Sports News Reviews* series.
    Released on April 29.
    (20 minutes)
    Warner Brothers

A Cavalcade of Girls (1950) D: Robert Youngson.
Entry in the *Vitaphone Varieties* series.
    Released on August 12.

(1 reel)
Warner Brothers

Blaze Busters (1950) D: Robert Youngson.
Narrated by Dwight Weist.
Looking back on how firefighters responded to famous conflagrations in past years. Produced by Robert Youngson. Entry in the *Vitaphone Varieties* series.
Academy Award Nomination: (Short Subject—One Reel) Robert Youngson.
Released on December 30.
(1 reel/sepia tone)
Warner Brothers

Horse-Hide Heroes (1951) D: Robert Youngson.
Narrated by Dwight Weist.
A lineup of notable baseball players from yesteryear.
Released on March 10.
(10 minutes)
Warner Brothers

World of Kids (1951) D: Robert Youngson.
Narrated by Dwight Weist.
The humorous side of children's recreation. Produced by Robert Youngson. Entry in the *Vitaphone Novelties* series.
Academy Award:
(Short Subject—One Reel) Robert Youngson.
Released on June 23.
(10 minutes)
Warner Brothers

Disaster Fighters (1951) D: Robert Youngson.
Narrated by Dwight Weist.
Footage of floods, hurricanes, and earthquakes from the archives of Pathé News. Entry in the *Vitaphone Varieties* series.
Released on August 11.
(10 minutes)
Warner Brothers

Lighter Than Air (1951) D: Robert Youngson.
Narrated by Dwight Weist.
   Reviewing the days of zeppelins, blimps, and dirigibles—including the construction of a hangar for such aircraft.
   Released on October 20.
   (1 reel)
   Warner Brothers

Animals Have All the Fun (1952) D: Robert Youngson.
Narrated by Ward Wilson.
   This series of clips from film archives demonstrate the comic abilities of the animal world.
   Released on April 18.
   (10 minutes)
   Warner Brothers

Daredevil Days (1952) D: Robert Youngson.
Narrated by Dwight Weist.
   The 1920s were a decade of silly and sometimes dangerous stunts, some captured on film and shown here.
   Released on August 9.
   (10 minutes)
   Warner Brothers

Too Much Speed (1952) D: Robert Youngson.
Narrated by Dwight Weist.
   Whether they are two-wheeled or four-wheeled, vehicles will always be subjected to races.
   Released in November.
   (11 minutes)
   Warner Brothers

No Adults Allowed (1953) D: Robert Youngson.
Children are once again in the spotlight.
   Released on April 11.
   (10 minutes)
   Warner Brothers

Head Over Heels (1953) D: Robert Youngson.
Narrated by Dwight Weist.
>Wintertime sports that take place in the mountains are the subject.
>Released on June 20.
>(10 minutes)
>Warner Brothers

Looking at Life (1953) D: Robert Youngson.
Some interesting views of Earth are presented, including from a rocket and from under the ocean. Also seen are some famous happenings and persons of yesteryear.
>Released on July 18.
>(20 minutes)
>Warner Brothers

Say It with Spills (1953) D: Robert Youngson.
Narrated by Andre Baruch.
>A look as some rough sports such as boxing and bullfighting.
>Released on October 24.
>(10 minutes)
>Warner Brothers

Magic Movie Moments (1953) D: Robert Youngson.
Narrated by Dwight Weist.
>As Warner Brothers prepares to re-release its 1928 film *Noah's Ark*, this short subject highlights scenes from the movie and shows clips of the original New York City premiere. Footage of George O'Brien, Dolores Costello, Paul McAllister, and Noah Beery Sr. Entry in the *Vitaphone Varieties* series.
>Released on December 26.
>(10 minutes)
>Warner Brothers

They Were Champions (1954) D: Robert Youngson.
Narrated by Dwight Weist.
>Footage of the leading boxers in sports history culled from film vaults.
>Released on January 24.
>(20 minutes)
>Warner Brothers

This Wonderful World (1954) D: Robert Youngson.
Narrated by Dwight Weist and Dan Donaldson.

Historic scenes and personalities clipped from the newsreel archives, Included are Theodore Roosevelt and a flood in Spain.

Released on March 27.
(20 minutes)
Warner Brothers

I Remember When (1954) D: Robert Youngson.
Narrated by Dwight Weist.

Old films show selected events in America from the 1890s through the 1910s. Seen are San Francisco's 1906 earthquake, flooding in Ohio during 1913, Theodore Roosevelt, an Easter parade on New York City's Fifth Avenue, the Wright Brothers, President Woodrow Wilson's inaugural parade. Entry in the *Vitaphone Varieties* series.

Released on April 3.
(10 minutes)
Warner Brothers

Thrills from the Past (1954) D: Robert Youngson.
Narrated by Dwight Weist.

Featurette fashioned around clips from the 1927 Warner Brothers melodrama *Old San Francisco*, with footage of Dolores Costello, Warner Oland, and Anna May Wong. Entry in the *Vitaphone Novelty* series. Produced by Robert Youngson.

Released on May 8.
(10 minutes)
Warner Brothers

When Sports Were King (1954) D: Robert Youngson.
Narrated by Dwight Weist.

A look at the giants of the 1920s sports world: Lou Gehrig and Babe Ruth (baseball); Harold 'Red' Grange (football); Knute Rockne (college football coach); Walter Hagen, Bobby Jones and Gene Sarazen (golf); Molla Mallory, William 'Big Bill' Tilden, and Helen Wills (tennis); jockey Earl Sande and racehorse Man o' War.

Released on June 19.
(10 minutes)
Warner Brothers

This Was Yesterday (1954) D: Robert Youngson.
Narrated by Dwight Weist.

The filmic spotlight falls on historic people of 1910s America: Sarah Bernhardt, William Jennings Bryan, Anna Case, Thomas A. Edison, Henry Ford, Warren G. Harding, Harry Lauder, General John J. Pershing, Franklin D. Roosevelt, Theodore Roosevelt, John Philip Sousa, Billy Sunday, and Pancho Villa.

Released on July 31.
(2 reels)
Warner Brothers

This Mechanical Age (1954) D: Robert Youngson.
Narrated by Dwight Weist.

The history of man's endeavors to fly. Produced by Robert Youngson.
Academy Award: (Short Subject—One Reel) Robert Youngson.
Released on August 28.
(10 minutes)
Warner Brothers

A Bit of the Best (1954) D: Robert Youngson.
Narrated by Dwight Weist.

Scenes from a Rin-Tin-Tin silent movie of the 1920s, with footage of the heroic German Shepherd, Virginia Brown Faire, and Jason Robards Sr.
Released on December 25.
(9 minutes)
Warner Brothers

Those Exciting Days (1955) D: Robert Youngson.
Narrated by Dwight Weist.

Views of Europe just prior to and during World War One.
Released on March 12.
(10 minutes)
Warner Brothers

When the Talkies Were Young (1955) D: Robert Youngson.
Narrated by Dwight Weist.

Scenes from five Warner Brothers pictures made during the early sound years.

- James Cagney and Joan Blondell in *Sinner's Holiday* (1930).
- Spencer Tracy and Bette Davis in *20,000 Years in Sing Sing* (1933).
- Edward G. Robinson and Boris Karloff in *Five Star Final* (1931).
- Barbara Stanwyck and Clark Gable in *Night Nurse* (1931).
- John Barrymore and Marian Marsh in *Svengali* (1931).

Also seen is Louis Calhern. Written and produced by Robert Youngson.
Released on April 29.
(20 minutes/DVD)
Warner Brothers

Fire, Wind and Flood (1955) D: Robert Youngson.
Narrated by Dwight Weist.
Films show the devastation of natural disasters. Entry in the *Warner Varieties* series.
Released on April 30.
(9 minutes)
Warner Brothers

Some of the Greatest (1955) D: Robert Youngson.
Narrated by Dwight Weist.
The 1926 film *Don Juan* is condensed to fit this one-reeler. Footage of John Barrymore, Mary Astor, Myrna Loy, Warner Oland, Estelle Taylor, and Montagu Love. Produced by Robert Youngson.
Released on July 18.
(10 minutes)
Warner Brothers

Gadgets Galore (1955) D: Robert Youngson.
Narrated by Ward Wilson and Dwight Weist.
The introductions and effects of automobiles in America, primarily racing. Footage of early racer Barney Oldfield and Russell Simpson as a man in the theater audience. Written and produced by Robert Youngson, who was also film editor.
Released on July 30.
(10 minutes)
Warner Brothers

An Adventure to Remember (1955) D: Robert Youngson.
Narrated by Dwight Weist.

Highlights from the 1923 silent film *Isle of Lost Ships*, with footage of Virginia Valli and Jason Robards Sr. Entry in the *Warner Novelty* series.

Released on October 1.

(9 minutes)

Warner Brothers

It Happened to You (1955) D: Robert Youngson.
Narrated by Jay Jackson.

A look at the home front and army life during World War One.

Released on December 31.

(18 minutes/RCA Sound)

Warner Brothers

Faster and Faster (1956) D: Robert Youngson.
Narrated by Dwight Weist.

Racing on the water, whether it be by sailboat or power craft.

Released in January.

(10 minutes)

Warner Brothers

The Picture Parade (1956) D: Robert Youngson.
Narrated by Dan Donaldson, Jay Jackson, and Dwight Weist.

A potpourri of people, animals, and the natural and man-made wonders of America.

Released on March 31.

(19 minutes/RCA Sound)

Warner Brothers

Crashing the Water Barrier (1956) D: Konstantin Kalser.
Donald Campbell, Leo Villa. Narrated by Jay Jackson.

Auto-racer Campbell switches from cars to powerboats as he pushes a jet craft to incredible speeds on Lake Meade, Nevada. Written by Reuven Frank. Produced by Konstantin Kalser with Robert Youngson as production supervisor. Entry in the *Sports Parade* series.

Academy Award:

(Short Subject—One Reel) Konstantin Kalser.

Released on April 15.

(9 minutes/RCA Sound/Warnercolor)
Warner Brothers

I Never Forget a Face (1956) D: (Robert Youngson).
Narrated by Ward Wilson, Dwight Weist.
  Some famous people of 1920s America are caught by the cameras: Presidential candidate Warren G. Harding runs his campaign from the porch of his house and gets Al Jolson to sing for the crowd; President Calvin Coolidge, who took office after Harding; the Democratic National Convention of 1920 spotlights William Jennings Bryan and vice presidential nominee Franklin Delano Roosevelt; the Prince of Wales visits; the famed 'Monkey Trial' of 1925 argued by William Jennings Bryan and Clarence Darrow; Richard E. Byrd prepares for his flight over the North Pole; English writer George Bernard Shaw comes to America. Also seen are Hiram Johnson, James M. Cox, Henry Ford, Thomas Edison, John Burroughs, Harvey Firestone, Prince Edward, Duke of York George VI, Lady Elizabeth Bowes-Lyon, Elizabeth II, John T. Scopes, Charles Lindbergh, Clarence Chamberlin, John D. Rockefeller, William Howard Taft, Alfred E. Smith, Grace Coolidge, Duchess of Windsor, and Queen Mary. Entry in the *Warner Specials* series. Written and produced by Robert Youngson.
  Academy Award Nomination: (Short Subject—One Reel) Robert Youngson.
  Released on April 28.
  (11 minutes)
  Warner Brothers

Through the Camera's Eye (1956) D: Robert Youngson.
Narrated by Dwight Weist.
  A segment about Washington Irving's Sleepy Hollow; how the world is viewed through a microscope; a series of giant telescopes.
  Released on August 11.
  (20 minutes)
  Warner Brothers

Animals and Kids (1956) D: Robert Youngson.
Narrated by Ward Wilson and Jay Jackson.
  Funny antics of critters and children.
  Released on August 18.

(10 minutes/RCA Sound)
Warner Brothers

Radio Appearances

The Film Art (WBAI-FM, dial 99.5, New York City), "Comedy Then and Now: Silent vs. Sound," April 17, 1960, 8 p.m. – 8:45 p.m.
   Host: Gideon Bachmann.
   Film producer-director Robert Youngson is interviewed.

Observation Point (WQXR-New York City, dial 1560 AM, 96.3 FM), September 4, 1964, 2:30 p.m. – 3 p.m.
   Host: Duncan MacDonald.
   Film producer Robert Youngson discusses past and present moviemaking.

Mimi Benzel (WNBC-New York City), September 23, 1964, 12:10 p.m. – 1:55 p.m.
   Host: Candy Jones
   Comedian Jack Benny and film producer Robert Youngson are interviewed.

Television Appearances

The Steve Allen Show **(NBC), December 22, 1957.**
   Stars: Steve Allen, Louis Nye, Tom Poston, Don Knotts. Announcer: Gene Rayburn. The Skitch Henderson Orchestra.
   Steve and guest Gertrude Berg do a supermarket shopping sketch in which Gertrude plays an excited fan. Film documentary producer Robert Youngson shows clips of past stars Stan Laurel and Oliver Hardy, Carole Lombard, and Will Rogers. Other guests include actor Tony Perkins, star of Broadway's *Look Homeward, Angel*; gospel singer Mahalia Jackson; opera singer George London; and the United Nations Choir. Written by Stan Burns, Don Hinkley, Mike Marmer, Frank Peppiatt, and Herb Sargent. *Broadcast in color.*
   Songs:
   Tony: "How About You?"

Mahalia: "Silent Night."
George, Choir: "A Mighty Fortress."

Discovery '63 (ABC), March 6, 1963.

Hosts: Virginia Gibson, Frank Buxton. Announcer: Bill Owen.

A look into the world of silent screen comedy. Robert Youngson, collector of old films—as well as a producer-director of various documentaries on silent cinema—presents clips of the era's funny stars: Buster Keaton, Charlie Chaplin, and the Keystone Kops.

www.ingramcontent.com/pod-product-compliance
Lightning Source LLC
Chambersburg PA
CBHW071434160426
43195CB00013B/1892